ONE WAY
TO SPELL MAN

by Wallace Stegner

NOVELS

All the Little Live Things
A Shooting Star
Second Growth
The Big Rock Candy Mountain
Fire and Ice
On a Darkling Plain
The Potter's House
Remembering Laughter
Joe Hill
Angle of Repose
The Spectator Bird
Recapitulation

SHORT STORIES

The City of the Living
The Women on the Wall

NONFICTION

Beyond the Hundredth Meridian
One Nation (with the editors of *Look*)
The Gathering of Zion
Mormon Country
Wolf Willow
The Sound of Mountain Water
The Uneasy Chair
The Letters of Bernard DeVoto

ONE WAY
TO SPELL MAN

Wallace Stegner

DOUBLEDAY & COMPANY, INC.
GARDEN CITY, NEW YORK
1982

ISBN: 0-385-17720-8
Library of Congress Catalog Card Number: 81-43428

Foreword Copyright © 1982 by Wallace Stegner
ALL RIGHTS RESERVED
PRINTED IN THE UNITED STATES OF AMERICA
FIRST EDITION

Acknowledgments

"This I Believe," edited by Edward P. Morgan, copyright © 1952 by Help, Inc. Renewed 1980. Reprinted by permission of Simon & Schuster, a Division of Gulf & Western Corporation. "One Way to Spell Man," copyright © 1958 by *Saturday Review*. All rights reserved. Reprinted with permission. "Fiction: A Lens on Life," copyright 1950 by *Saturday Review*. Copyright © renewed 1978 by *Saturday Review*. All rights reserved. Reprinted with permission. "To a Young Writer," copyright © 1959 by Wallace Stegner. "The Writer and the Concept of Adulthood," copyright © 1976 by the American Academy of Arts and Sciences. Reprinted by permission. "Excellence and the Pleasure Principle," from *Writing*, Vol. 1, Nos. 3 & 4. "Good-bye to All T–t!" copyright © 1965 by Wallace Stegner. "That New Man, the American," copyright © 1973 by Stanford Alumni Association. "The Provincial Consciousness" appeared first in the Summer 1974 issue of *The University of Toronto Quarterly*. Given by permission. "The West Coast: Region with a View," copyright © 1959 by *Saturday Review*. All rights reserved. Reprinted with permission. "Making a Myth," first published as an Introduction to *My Dear Wister—The Frederick Remington–Owen Wister Letters*, by Ben Vorpahl, copyright © 1972 by American West Publishing Company. By permission of Crown Publishers, Inc. "A. B. Guthrie," Wallace Stegner's Introduction to *The Big Sky*, by A. B. Guthrie. Copyright 1947, and © renewed by A. B. Guthrie. Reprinted by permission of Houghton Mifflin Company. "Walter Clark's Frontier," copyright © 1973 by Wallace Stegner. "A Desert Shelf," copyright © 1977 by Wallace Stegner. "Ansel Adams and the Search for Perfection," reprinted by permission of publisher from *Ansel Adams: Images 1923–1974*. Copyright © 1974, 1981 by the Trustees of the Ansel Adams Publishing Rights Trust. Foreword by Wallace Stegner. Boston: New York Graphic Society. "The Gift of Wilderness" first appeared in *New West Magazine* as "Apples and Oranges" and "The Call of the Wild," copyright © 1981 by Wallace Stegner.

Contents

Foreword

The essays collected here were written over a period of thirty years, from the early 1950s to day before yesterday. All of those in the first section, as well as some of those in the second, are exercises in belief, pitons driven into the cracked granite of uncertainty to establish a temporary foothold. On reading them over, I do not find the assumptions from which they proceed or the attitudes they arrive at either very bizarre or very new, but I do not apologize for that. In a reasonably long life, one learns how little novelty actually matters, and how brief is its duration.

In a time when it is mildly embarrassing to admit to any beliefs at all, or any standards of conduct or aesthetics, I am somewhat surprised to find that having lived through the 1910s, 1920s, 1930s, 1940s, 1950s, 1960s, and 1970s I retain most of the attitudes expressed in these trial syntheses made along the way. Some of them I find naïve, some are illustrated out of the works of writers whom I have by now all but forgotten. But the attitudes, the essential code, I would not change. Coming from nowhere into this culture, I had to struggle to know who I was; and looking backward at these expressions of myself, I have to say all over again, "Yes, this I believe, this I will stick with, or am stuck with."

Belief and attitude form the base from which one projects a life and the writing which is its by-product. The accidents of geography, region, nation, race provide the raw material for both. The second group of essays in this collection are attempts at identification and definition in terms of the region that bred me, the West. I have tried to define it not so much as it has affected my own writing, though that would not be difficult, but as it gives point and particularity to those assumptions and attitudes dealt with in the first group of essays, and as it has produced, in the writers and artists of the region, trial syntheses of another kind, whole men such as Ansel Adams, whose art is an affirmation of life, as their country and their region have given them to know it.

PART I

*This I Believe**

It is terribly difficult to say honestly, without posing or faking, what one truly and fundamentally believes. Reticence or an itch to make public confession may distort or dramatize what is really there to be said, and public expressions of belief are so closely associated with inspirational activity, and in fact so often stem from someone's desire to buck up the downhearted and raise the general morale, that belief becomes an evangelical matter.

In all honesty, what I believe is neither inspirational nor evangelical. Passionate faith I am suspicious of, because it hangs and burns witches and heretics, and generally I am more in sympathy with the witches and heretics than with the sectarians who hang and burn them. I fear immoderate zeal—Christian, Moslem, Communist, or whatever—because it restricts the range of human understanding and the wise reconciliation of human differences, and creates an orthodoxy with a sword in its hand.

It is impossible to claim that I am even a sound Christian, though the code of conduct to which I subscribe was preached more eloquently by Jesus Christ than by any other. About God I simply do not know; I don't think I *can* know. That limits my beliefs to the conduct of this life.

However far I have missed achieving it, I know that modera-

* From Ed Murrow's radio program This I Believe.

tion is one of the virtues I most believe in. But I believe as well
in a whole catalogue of Christian and classical virtues: in
kindness and generosity, in steadfastness, in courage, and much
else. I believe further that good depends not on things but on
the use we make of things. Everything potent, from human
love to atomic energy, is dangerous; it produces ill about as
readily as good; it becomes good only through the control, the
discipline, the wisdom with which we use it. Much of this control is social, a thing which laws and institutions and uniforms
enforce, but much of it must be personal, and I do not see how
we can evade the obligation to take full responsibility for what
we individually do. Our reward for self-control and the acceptance of private responsibility is not usually money or power.
Self-respect and the respect of others are quite enough.

All this is to say that I believe in conscience, not as something implanted by divine act but as something learned since
infancy from tradition and the society which has bred us. The
outward forms of virtue will vary greatly from nation to nation.
A Chinese scholar of the old school or an Indian raised on the
Vedas and the Bhagavad-Gita has a conscience that will differ
from mine. But in the essential outlines of what constitutes
human decency we vary amazingly little. The Chinese and the
Indian know as well as I do what kindness is, what generosity
is, what fortitude is. They can define justice quite as accurately.
It is only when they and I are blinded by tribal and denomina-
tional narrowness that we insist on our differences and can recognize goodness only in the robes of our own crowd.

A man is a great enough creature and a great enough enigma
to deserve both our pride and our compassion, and engage our
fullest sense of mystery. I shall certainly never do as much with
my life as I want to, and I shall sometimes fail miserably to live
up to my conscience, but I shall not mistrust its word, even
when I can't obey it. I am terribly glad to be alive; and when I
have wit enough to think about it, terribly proud to be a man
and an American, with all the rights and privileges that those
words connote; and most of all I am humble before the responsibilities that are also mine. For no right comes without a responsibility, and being born luckier than most of the world's
millions, I am also born more obligated.

One Way
to Spell Man

Sinclair Lewis's old bacteriologist Max Gottlieb told young Martin Arrowsmith that the only sure thing in this life is the quantitative method. Perhaps he was right. The empirical process needs no defense. Hypothesis, experiment, and verification have lengthened our lives, shrunk our globe, idled our hands, replaced our legs with wheels, created pills to galvanize our inertia and pills to soothe our hysteria, dictated the classifications in our bird books and the alloys in our burglar alarms, told us what crops to plant and what weathers to expect, synthesized our insect sprays and toughened the fiber of our insects, made clear the material structure of the universe, taken the natural virtues out of our foods, put synthetic virtues back into them, and shaped the intellectual and physical life of nearly everyone. No one in these days is in any real danger of underestimating the importance of the quantitative method. The danger is precisely the reverse. Because the method *is* sure, because it has proved effective in so many things, we may be (and some of us clearly are) deluded into thinking that it can do anything, that there is no sort of question it cannot ultimately answer.

It is preposterous to stand up seriously and assert the validity of the arts as a means to truth; and yet one probably needs to, at least against those who do not think but whose collective thoughtlessness is made, by stochastic processes, to represent and even guide public opinion. We hear so often, sounding under the cry for more mathematicians and more engineers, the positivist and pragmatist scorn for the arts and literature as "frills," the contemptuous conviction that tradition is 90 percent argument in support of error. Art and literature, we understand, are charming (for those who like such things) survivals, hangovers from the days of witchcraft and wonder, and science will sooner or later render them unnecessary.

There is probably a real quarrel between the arts and technology—what could Vermeer make of a General Electric kitchen? —but surely there is none between art and science, nor between their respective intentions and methods. Science does not represent a system that will ultimately freeze art and the other witchcrafts out, but a method that supplements, and will always need supplementing by, the artist's ancient and unverifiable insights. There are questions that science not only cannot answer but doesn't know how to ask; there are kinds of truth with which it should not concern itself and which, if it does concern itself with them, go dead in its hands. The world, as John Foxe remarked in *The Book of Martyrs*, is a vast nursery, and men are children engaged in trying to spell God with the wrong blocks. In that effort, necessarily doomed to failure, the arts are as important as the vowels are in the alphabet. We do not help by asking our children to spell God with nothing but the consonants of science.

As a system, as a bent of mind, science aims at the understanding of the material world. Along with everything else, it examines man himself, dissects his tissues, tinkers with his endocrines, measures the electrical discharges of his brain, scrutinizes the effect upon him of personality-changing drugs, classifies his physical and psychic types, by cybernetics imitates his thought processes, and by photosynthesis tries to reproduce the very life that animates him. It is entirely proper that it should do all these things, and more. Anything that can be quantified ought to be quantified, everything that will submit to scientific measure ought to be measured, and there is no way of telling what will submit until the attempt has been made. But this does not mean that all the results of all the sciences, no matter how much we learn of the endocrines and the brain, no matter if we project ourselves into space or clear out of our proper order of magnitude, no matter if we reproduce life in laboratories, will render art unnecessary or prove it invalid. One has a certain faith that even the black boxes, the robots, and the other golems of the investigators will by some trick of feedback or induced current learn to evade control and develop consciousness, emotions, and inevitably art. Science will not have made man or life complete until some robot rudely draws a transformer or an insulator on the laboratory wall.

Art is the record of man acting, man as aware experience; and though scientific discovery may well modify it by modifying man himself, it seems likely to affect only the forms, never the essence. As Albert Camus has said, in art "a profound thought is in a constant state of becoming. It adopts the experience of a life and assumes its shape." No scientific advance, and no subsequent art either, really affects it. Atomic weapons do not make Homer unreadable; Copernicus, Newton, and Sir James Jeans have not taken the poetic truth out of *Paradise Lost*; Ibsen does not replace Shakespeare, any more than Shakespeare replaced Aeschylus. And here lies one of the differences between art and science. For Harvey *did* do irreparable harm to the medical science of Galen; and Einstein, Urey, Fermi, Bohr, and company have taken a great deal of the order out of Newton's universe. The fact is, "progress" is not a word that is very useful in art. While science proceeds from imperfect or disproved hypotheses to new hypotheses, from synthesis to higher synthesis, art may in its very beginnings arrive at some of the highest expressions of its own peculiar sort of truth. The bulls on the cave walls of Lascaux were masterpieces when they were painted, more than fifteen thousand years ago, and they remain masterpieces. There, from the dawn of the species, looks out at us a spirit that jolts us with the recognition of our shared humanity.

And so if one is driven to say a word for the humanities and the arts in a time when too much ill-considered technocratic noise pretends to be the "voice of science," one is not speaking against science or scientists, but only for sanity. Science and art are complementary, not competing. And it would be idiotic to defend the arts for pseudoscientific or pragmatic reasons, for any "usefulness" as "communication" or "therapy" or anything else that they may incidentally have. They are indispensable precisely because they are expressions of truth, a way of understanding, at the deepest level, the world of man.

At their most creative edge, science and art both represent original questionings—pure research—and both rely upon a galvanizing and originating intuition. It is in their proofs that they differ. When scientific research has succeeded, moreover, and has reached the stage of public verification, it is open to exploitation as technology, whose function is the reproduction of useful goods. But when art has unveiled some truth and it has become everybody's property and the method of its unveiling is part of everybody's technique, its name is stereotype, and stereotype is not valuable in artistic matters, whatever it may be in an industrial world dedicated to mass production with interchangeable parts. Artistic insights tend to remain discrete; they do not necessarily make the building blocks of future insights; the tradition accumulates less by accrual than by deviation and rebellion.

And when a science and an art accost the same materials, the same apparent problems, it becomes very clear that they ask different kinds of questions. Examine a piece of literature in the light of communications theory: Pose it as a model communications system, strive for the equation that will express its entropy, get all the reluctant variables under control, and measure the intellectual and emotional output against the intellectual and emotional input; you may have demonstrated something, even something important, about something, but not about literature as an art. For it is of the essence of art that it is different things to different people. Within certain fluid boundaries of general meaning and feeling, a writer is, as Robert Frost has said, entitled to anything a reader can find in him.

And when the creative process itself is put under examination, as it has been at the University of California, strange findings may emerge and strange conflicts arise. I believe that the clinical examiners there have found writers their most recalcitrant and difficult subjects: they do not often cooperate, they question the questioners, they doubt the method, they repudiate the purpose, they cling jealously to their *Geist* and their *mystique.*

The point is, they are normally interested not at all in the creative process, whatever that may be. The process is to them only the loose collection of skills and habits and witchcrafts and prayers, best not examined too closely, by which they manage to keep "a profound thought in a constant state of becoming." So when an examiner shoves a box of alphabetical blocks across a desk to Frank O'Connor and asks him to demonstrate, using the blocks as elements of raw material and structure, how he "builds" or creates a story, she has from a writer's point of view earned O'Connor's reply: that he quit playing with blocks when he was three. What he is trying to spell in his stories, whether "God" or "man" or any other small difficult word, is not spellable in such terms as the blocks imply, and is not susceptible to the quantitative or mensurative or statistical methods of social science. It is precisely because they *are* creative, and not statistical, that the writers have given the clinicians trouble.

Art is all variables, all particulars—and yet at the moment of meeting, both work and reader must operate as wholes and must collaboraté toward meaning. The total experience of his life, conscious, unconscious, pre- and postnatal, is potentially involved when Frank O'Connor writes a story. To read it right, a reader must bring the same sort of wholeness, the same sort of attention, to his response. It seems to me clear that systematic analysis is not the proper reading method—certainly not the whole final method. A difficult work may require some preliminary dissection, and analysis after the meeting of work and reader may help the reader clarify his own response and the qualities he responds to. But the response, like the work itself, eludes final analysis; and to see how inconclusive even the most sustained, elaborate, and cunning critical analysis is, consult the history of the criticism of any great literary work, say *Hamlet.*

The play remains free, with a solid reality of its own, as mysterious as life and much more enduring. "Humanity," says one of Isak Dinesen's characters, "the men and women of this earth, are only the plaster of God, and we, the artists, are His tools, and when the statue is finished in marble or bronze, He breaks us all up. When you die you will probably go out like a candle, with nothing left, but in the mansions of eternity will walk Orlando, the Misanthrope, and my Donna Elvira."

What anyone who speaks for art must be prepared to assert is the validity of nonscientific experience and the seriousness of nonverifiable insight. The second is the easier. For nearly a hundred years now, literature has assumed for some people the spiritual responsibilities traditionally belonging to religion. Literature has become for many of us, as it became for the father of William Butler Yeats and many of his generation, the source of wisdom and the receptacle of values. But at the risk of flogging a corpse, let us summarize a hypothetical hostile point of view. We may borrow the corpse from Philip Wheelwright and Eliseo Vivas, and it is such a corpse as deserves to be flogged. As Wheelwright and Vivas describe what they call "semantic positivism," it assumes that

1) Literary observations and insights are unverified, hence unverifiable, and hence always inferior to insights obtained through the experimental method.

2) Emotion is the essential element that distinguishes poetic from scientific matters; emotions are merely unformed ideas; hence the essential nature of poetic insight is both subjective and vague, hence unreliable, hence inferior.

3) There are two kinds of language, one rigorous, denotative, semantically aseptic, suitable for science (compare Professor Bloomfield's "Mathematics is the best that language can do"), and the other connotative, associative, and subjective, suitable for poetry. Science uses language "purely," aspiring toward the precision of mathematics; poetry, on the other hand, "exploits ambiguity."

There are numerous things about that hypothetical position that one would like to comment on, particularly the implicit justification it contains for all the dialects of behavioral-science jargon. But what is more important here, clearly, is that if we accept this position we tacitly accept the secondary status, and eventually the withering away, of all religion, all metaphysics, most philosophy, much history, and even some branches of mathematics. Or we shall have to admit that these varieties of human experience are merely entertaining, without relation to the truth as men can know it. Or we shall have to look upon them as residual and doomed, like the belief in poltergeists and the rites of Astarte. Or we shall have to compromise by saying that much is unknowable even by the most imaginative applications of the experimental method, and that art, religion, and metaphysics are ritual or systematic formulations of unknowability, the best we can do with these refractory subjects under the circumstances.

Possibly the arts may be very often merely entertaining, remote from the profounder truth, and entangled in ritual. But at their best they are a perfectly valid instrument of knowledge: knowledge of things *as experienced,* knowledge of which both observed and observer make a part. If they were not, we could not be jolted across fifteen millennia by the marvelous rightness of those bulls of Lascaux, by the way in which, through capturing one image of movement and power, a naked caveman has managed to suggest infinite possibilities of movement and power and the incurable wonder of life.

What is added to brute fact by art is something like what is added to the bumblebee to permit him to fly. Aerodynamically it is impossible that a bumblebee should fly; in experience, he buzzes by your ear.

Art is neither conceptual nor propositional. Its truths are not the truths of experiment, nor yet the propositions of deductive logic. It does not deal in such generalizations as "All men are liars." It deals in individual liars. Like all the arts, literature is exemplary, it proceeds iconically, it arrives not at general concepts but at what Wheelwright and perhaps others have called "concrete universals." Its truth is conceptualized in the union of work and reader; it is an insight communicated by example from writer to reader. Also, it inevitably takes some coloration from the reader's temperament and state of mind and cultural background. It is a collaboration, a meeting of minds and spirits, a thing that lights up like love. It gets much of its virtue, as its detractors assert, from a controlled ambiguity. It does not state. It imitates or reflects, and is witnessed.

As there is truth in the charge that poetry deals in ambiguities, so there is truth in the assertion that art is not "objective." It never is. It may *pretend* to be, for purposes of its own, but it should never *try* to be. A literary masterpiece involves the presence of two temperaments (and sometimes, between them as guide or catalyst or obfuscator, the critic). It is incurably iconic, but not objective; a better adjective would be "clear-eyed." The artist himself is a lens to see through, and I cannot see how the worth of any work of art can be based upon anything but the testing—by the best audiences over a considerable period of time—of the artist's insight. The proof of art, in other words, is in the response, in the aesthetic experience. By no means all artists are dependable, but neither are all audiences. Art is one of the most wasteful of human activities, filled with trial and error, nonsense, failure, unjust neglect, pretension, indifference, and the sad inadequacy of the human instrument.

But in the rare instances when the human instrument is clear-eyed, the linguistic instrument evocative, and the audience adequate, who will deny that literature can bring us truths: real truths, truths in solution, buried in their contexts, embedded and implicit in their created worlds, truths exemplified, unabstracted, concrete, demanding our participation? The truths of literature possess an enduring ability to satisfy or at least allay human questioning, and they have every right to be called profound, though work and process and maker and response are all outside the possibility of full test or measurement.

A system which agrees, as the experimental method does, to exclude all emotion, gains its special and valuable kind of truth by limiting the possibilities of interruption or interference or contradiction. It gains one kind of truth at the expense of another kind. Art, by contrast, gives up any claim to verifiability, gives up limited and controlled truth, in exchange for its truth-in-context, truth by confrontation and recognition. It assumes that these relationships are a part of the human mixture, to be ignored at the observer's peril; and that they are not only a vital part of human life but a part of the means of full communication, an indispensable instrument of understanding. Anyone who would look upon them as merely "unformed ideas" would be capable of asking Frank O'Connor to build a story out of blocks.

Finally, far from yearning toward a semantically aseptic language, a writer who is also an artist must make use of all the cultural moss that words gather, all the suggestive coloration and patina of language. He does indeed, in this sense, "exploit ambiguity," but that phrase itself is a sample of how difficult it is to force language toward absolute precision. Look at the word "exploit," with its hint of scorn, its suggestion of the pejorative. It comes, by way of Old French, from the past participle of the Latin verb *explicare*, to unfold or display. It has come a long way from its origins, and on its way it has acquired beyond erasure the smudge of baseness, bad motives, opportunism. It is not a word for a semantic positivist to use against poetry unless he is willing to use poetry's own methods.

It is precisely the patina of language that gives an artist in words his power and his subtlety. He would as soon think of cutting bread with a sunbeam as try to use language with the precision of mathematics. He is after a much more complex, much more subtle kind of precision, if it can be called precision at all. The right word may be located by its sound, or by some flicker of momentary association, quite as often as by its denotative accuracy; and it does not exist in itself, a single thing, a single meaning; it exists in total entanglement with other words, with truth by evocation and response. It assumes the view that emotions are a tone and a style, in adjustment to situation and character and mood. Words used poetically are a medium as fluid as watercolors, and some of the best effects may seem accidental even to the man who creates them. He does not have to know, with his conscious mind, exactly what he is doing. He is fishing in obscure depths, he is a dealer in mysteries, a witch doctor not always easy with the forces he evokes but acutely aware of them while they are present.

Put another way, literature is a game played between writer and reader, who must be products of essentially similar cultures and traditions. In the jargon of behavioral science, literature is inevitably, even triumphantly, culture-bound. It is not verifiable knowledge; its tests are recognition and concurrence. In Anatole France's phrase, "Time alone makes masterpieces." But if literature is not "knowledge" in the scientific sense, it is a clarified, ordered, selected, and purified model of life, complete with the values that life evolves and preserving even the distressingly awkward variables. It is built on a framework of symbolic conventions, but it is the farthest thing from arbitrary, even when it experiments or revolts.

André Malraux has asserted, in the teeth of romantic doctrine, that art is learned not from nature but from other artists, and to the extent that all art develops conventional symbols, he cannot be argued with. Even what we think of as self-evident in any art tradition is likely to be the product of the long-shared-and-communicated learning that distinguishes man from all other animals. To take an example from painting, the mere fact of representation in two dimensions has to be learned. People of some tribes, I have read, are unable to recognize photographs of themselves. And I have put a dog to watch Disney's *The African Lion* on television and elicited only yawns. He can be scared out of his feeble wits by coming unexpectedly upon a stuffed dog, but the television lions do not scare him. They are only flickers of light. He hasn't learned the first principle of representational art.

But if art is in good part tradition, its truths, being linked with response, are the kind that will vary in kind or intensity with different responders. More than that, the most extreme rebellions by artists against their traditions are both possible and desirable. Picasso's violences against perspective, like Schoenberg's against key signatures and Faulkner's against syntax, are as radical as if in medicine some research doctor had declared against the germ theory of disease, and yet they are vital, healthy, and necessary. They assert the fullest freedom to question experience in any terms.

Any work of art is the product of a total human being commenting with his total understanding on experiences that with luck may become symbolically representative of larger experience, even of all experience. In literature, success is by no means a matter of mere verbal felicity: "The gift of words," said Conrad, who fortunately had it, "is no such great matter." A man is not made a hunter or a warrior by the mere possession of a firearm. And it cannot be said too often that there is no single explanation for a poem or story or novel, nor is explanation necessarily understanding, nor is understanding necessarily enjoyment. The simple necessities of pedagogy or a mistaken avidity for "ideas" may lead teachers and critics to confuse analysis with understanding. But what is vital is the aesthetic experience, never quite communicable, a collaborative act; and I can think of no better expression of what is involved in it than Conrad's preface, well known but not well known enough, to *The Nigger of the "Narcissus."* The artist, he says, unlike the thinker and the scientist, does not speak "authoritatively to our common sense and our intelligence." Instead,

> . . . confronted by the same enigmatical spectacle the artist descends within himself and in that lonely region of stress and strife, if he be deserving and fortunate, he finds the terms of his appeal. His appeal is made to our less obvious capacities: to that part of our nature which, because of the warlike conditions of existence, is necessarily kept out of sight within the more resisting and hard qualities—like the vulnerable body within a steel armour. His appeal is less loud, more profound, less distinct, more stirring—and sooner forgotten. Yet its effect endures forever. The changing wisdom of successive generations discards ideas, questions facts, demolishes theories. But the artist appeals to that part of our being which is not dependent on wisdom: to that in us which is a gift and not an acquisition—and, therefore, more permanently enduring. He speaks to our capacity for delight and wonder, to the sense of mystery surrounding our lives; to our sense of pity, and beauty, and pain; to the

latent feeling of fellowship with all creation—and to
the subtle but invincible conviction of solidarity that
knits together the loneliness of innumerable hearts, to
the solidarity in dreams, in joy, in sorrow, in aspirations, in illusions, in hope, in fear, which binds men
to each other, which binds together all humanity—the
dead to the living and the living to the unborn.

It is that which we respond to in the arts—that spark which,
as Eliot says, can leap twenty-five hundred years, the recognition of fellow humanity which art gives us more plainly than
life generally does, the "profound thought in a constant state
of becoming" which "adopts the experience of a life and assumes its shape." And if we are ever tempted to write or read
by the rules of the quantitative method, if we ever approach literature as if it were "subject matter," we would do well to
remind ourselves that the love and appreciation of literature
come by exposure, by a meeting, not through paraphrase or
explication. We could do worse than quote Conrad again,
speaking for the single, simple, and all-important thing that he
knew he must do as an artist:

> My task which I am trying to achieve is, by the power
> of the written word to make you hear, to make you
> feel—it is, before all, to make you *see*. That—and no
> more—and it is everything. If I succeed, you shall find
> there according to your deserts: encouragement, con-
> solation, fear, charm—all you demand—and perhaps,
> also that glimpse of truth for which you have forgot-
> ten to ask.

It is art's trick to approach experience through the senses and
to create a little world. This is perhaps to spell man by the
flash-card method rather than by analytic syllabification. Or
perhaps it isn't a way to *spell* man at all. Perhaps it is a way of
greeting him, an act of presentation and recognition.

It would be the wildest folly to think of reducing art to the
laws and the orderlinesses that are the ideal and monumental
strength of science. Only a Philistine would even attempt to do

it. For art reduced to law and order is only cliché; and it cannot be predicted, because it cannot be born until it *is* born. Creation, says Ezra Pound, is what has not yet found its way into language—into any language.

But once said, once created, it speaks truth to us. Literature, alive, gets its strength from the sense it communicates of intimate acquaintance and fellowship, from our acknowledgment, in response to the work of art's illumination, of things as they are.

Fiction:
A Lens on Life

The editor of a mass-circulation magazine once told me proudly that all through the Depression he had published not one story dealing with the Depression's peculiar problems. No unemployment, no flophouses, no breadlines, no despair. Nonfiction articles by the dozen dealt with these things, but stories and serials, no. Fiction was for fun, not for illumination. Fiction was phenobarbital, not amphetamine. And even "quality" magazines, which presumably have other views of fiction, are not entirely uninfluenced by considerations of escape. I have known such a magazine, one of the best published in the United States, to refuse a story that every editor on the staff was enthusiastic about, and to refuse it only because it dealt with a woman dying of cancer. The magazine's audience contained a good many elderly women, and fiction should not touch their fears.

The kind of fiction which, approvingly or otherwise, may be called lies is outside the present discussion. It is fiction as truth that I am concerned with here, fiction that reflects experience instead of escaping it, that stimulates instead of deadening. Serious fiction, so called, is written by a different kind of writer and for a different audience. It differs in intention, in materials, in method, and in its final effect. If it entertains—as it must—it entertains at a higher intellectual and emotional level; if it deals in make-believe—as it likewise must—it creates a make-believe world in order to comment on the real one. Serious fiction is not necessarily great and not even necessarily literature, because the talents of its practitioners may not be as dependable as their intentions. But all literature, including the great, will be written in this spirit.

The difference between the writer of serious fiction and the writer of escape entertainment is the clear difference between the artist and the craftsman. The one has the privilege and the faculty of original design; the other does not. The man who works from blueprints is a thoroughly respectable character, but he is of another order from the man who makes the blueprints in the first place.

The word "artist" is not a word I like. It has been adopted by crackpots and abused by pretenders and debased by people with talent but no humility. In its capital-A form it is the hallmark of that peculiarly repulsive sin of arrogance by which some practitioners of the arts retaliate for public neglect or compensate for personal inadequacy. I use it here only because there is no other word for the serious "maker" in words or stone or sound or colors.

Joseph Conrad once outlined the qualifications for the serious artist in a little essay called simply "Books." He said:

> A novelist who would think himself of a superior essence to other men would miss the first condition of his calling. To have the gift of words is no such great matter. A man furnished with a long-range weapon does not become a hunter or a warrior by the mere possession of a firearm; many other qualities of character and temperament are necessary to make him either one or the other. Of him from whose armory of phrases one in a hundred thousand may perhaps hit the far-distant and elusive mark of art I would ask that in his dealings with mankind he should be capa-

ble of giving a tender recognition to their obscure virtues. I would not have him impatient with their small
failings and scornful of their errors. I would not have
him expect too much gratitude from that humanity
whose fate, as illustrated in individuals, it is open to
him to depict as ridiculous or terrible. I would wish
him to look with a large forgiveness at men's ideas
and prejudices, which are by no means the outcome
of malevolence, but depend on their education, their
social status, even their professions. . . . I would wish
him to enlarge his sympathies by patient and loving
observation while he grows in mental power. It is in
the impartial practice of life, if anywhere, that the
promise of perfection for his art can be found, rather
than in the absurd formulas trying to prescribe this or
that particular method of technique or conception.
Let him mature the strength of his imagination
among the things of this earth. . . .

It is the job of this serious artist to bring order where no
order was before him or at least where his own special kind of
order was not. He has for material the whole of his experience,
actual and vicarious, and the wider and deeper it is, the better.
The more it has hurt him, short of actual crippling, the better.
The more he has enjoyed it, the better. But this experience by
which he estimates the experience of men at large is always
disorderly and contradictory and in our times is apt to be an
utter chaos. What he does to it is to shape it in patterns of
words that are idea and image and character. Somewhere in the
morass of his world he tramples out a foothold, or, to change
the figure, he bounds the panoramic and bewildering view with
his squared hands. The most inclusive vision is not necessarily
his aim; it is the *clearest* vision he is after, and this may involve
squinting or shutting one eye or even bending over and looking
at the view upside down through his spraddled legs, Japanese
fashion. However he does it—and his method is his own business—he tries with every piece of fiction, even the slightest
short story, to "create a world." The phrase is Conrad's, the job

is the endlessly repeated and endlessly new job of every serious writer. Every piece of fiction is thus not the application of a formula, not a neat and workmanlike job of joining and fitting, not an exercise in cleverness, but a trial of the writer's whole understanding and a reflection of his whole feeling and knowing.

Because he writes fiction in order to reflect or illuminate life, his materials obviously must come out of life. These materials are people, places, things—especially people. If fiction isn't people it is nothing, and so any fiction writer is obligated to be to some degree a lover of his fellowmen, though he may, like the Mormon preacher, love some of them a damn sight better than others. The people of his stories and novels will be, inevitably but in altered shapes, the people he himself has known. The flimsy little protestations that mark the front gate of every novel, the solemn statements that any resemblance to real persons living or dead is entirely coincidental, are fraudulent every time. A writer has no other material to make his people from than the people of his experience. If there is no resemblance to any real person, living or dead, the character is going to be pretty unconvincing. The only thing the writer can do is to recombine parts, suppress some characteristics and emphasize others, put two or three people into one fictional character, and pray the real-life prototypes won't sue.

The fiction writer is an incorrigible lover of concrete *things*. He has to build fiction out of such materials as the hard knotting of anger in the solar plexus, the hollowness of a night street, the sound of poplar leaves. In a contentious preface to a World War II Italian novel, Ernest Hemingway put it for the whole tribe:

> A writer finds rain [by which he means reality] to be made of knowledge, experience, wine, bread, oil, salt, vinegar, bed, early mornings, nights, days, the sea, men, women, dogs, beloved motor cars, bicycles, hills and valleys, the appearance and disappearance of trains on straight and curved tracks . . . cock grouse drumming on a basswood log, the smell of sweet grass and fresh smoked leather and Sicily.

By his very profession, a serious fiction writer is a vendor of the sensuous particulars of life, a perceiver and handler of things. His most valuable tools are his senses and his memory; what happens in his mind is primarily pictures. He is not ordinarily or ideally a generalizer, not a dealer in concepts, though some writers have tried to intellectualize fiction in this way under the impression that they were making it more respectable.

Ideas, of course, have a place in fiction, and any writer of fiction needs a mind. But ideas are not the best *subject matter* for fiction. They do not dramatize well. They are, rather, a byproduct, something the reader himself is led to formulate after watching the story unfold. The ideas, the generalizations, ought to be implicit in the selection and arrangement of the people and places and actions. They ought to haunt a piece of fiction as a ghost flits past an attic window after dark.

Any good serious fiction is collected out of reality, and its parts ought to be vivid and true to fact and to observation. The parts are reassembled in such a way that the architecture, the shape of the action, is meaningful. And if the fiction is good enough, that meaning will stretch, the building will throw a shadow longer than itself, the particular will become representative, general, symbolic, indefinitely applicable to other people, other situations. The writer's meaning is thus not a single or inert thing. It expands, it becomes part of the living thought of its readers. And it is this capacity for generalized meaning that gives serious fiction its illuminating and liberating effect. But no fiction should be asked to state its meaning flatly, in conceptual terms, any more than a ghost should be called upon to come out and stand a physical examination.

The methods a writer uses to arrive at this kind of meaning are relatively unimportant except to himself. Different writers will always get their foothold in reality in different ways, different places. Every generation finds its own way of speaking out, says Gertrude Stein. No classic looks anything like any classic that has preceded it, says Hemingway. The important writer will be recognizable not by new materials but by new insights, says V. S. Pritchett.

It is often necessary for a writer to distort the particulars of experience in order to see them better. As was remarked earlier, he can look upside down or squint or put on gauze spectacles or do what he chooses, so long as his method lets him see at least part of his world more clearly. To take only one example, the padded nightmare world of Franz Kafka represents a new insight. The solemnly logical course of the incredible begets a new satire and a new humor, and for all its strangeness Kafka's fiction reflects real men and real institutions better than many more-representational kinds of fiction.

Whatever the method, it will involve a simplification. By inexorable necessity, all art simplifies. Hemingway, learning to write "beginning with the simplest things," stripping his vocabulary to the bare Anglo-Saxon, reducing his sentences to the simple declarative, eliminating all latinate complexity, and trying to eliminate even such customary "cheating" as metaphor, simplifying his people and simplifying his themes, peeling down even his favorite theme of death to its simplest and most violent forms, represents only one kind, an extreme kind, of artistic simplification. The world that results in Hemingway's fiction may not be a world we like, but it is unmistakably a world. Conrad's world, in its own way, is just as simplified. Often it is a world within one ship, its deck the whole earth and its crew all mankind, and the moral universe bending over the actions of his people as close or as remote as the stars at sea. Even Henry James, on the surface one of the most complex and hairsplitting and qualifying and entangled of fictionists, begins with absolutely sweeping simplifications. To clear the way for the unimpeded moral choices which form the crucial moments of all his stories, he first eliminates most of what some other novelists might build their whole books from. No James character ever has to worry about making a living; James endows them all with handy inheritances. No James character is fettered by family responsibilities or any of the complex nets that fasten about the feet of people in life. All of James's people are free to move at will through the world he has made for them, absolutely and deliberately set free from all mundane entanglements so that their moral choices can be "pure" and uninfluenced. And though the complexities of the actual choice, the backing and filling, the delicate hesitancies and withholdings, the partial renunciations and the hair-fine scruples, may be almost maddeningly complex, the act of simplification which has made this complexity possible is just as impressive.

Any simplification the artist chooses is legitimate; it can be judged only on pragmatic grounds, by its success. Every writer is a blind man feeling the elephant, and even a great writer is likely to be limited in what he understands. His fictional world will reflect the special understandings he has. The world of Chekhov, in which unhappy people walk gray, muddy roads or ferry exiles like themselves across leaden Siberian rivers or take a moment's wry enjoyment from a wistful and frustrated life, is valid and recognizable; so is the world Tom Lea creates in *The Brave Bulls*, where man's confrontation of the immortal Terror takes the shape of the ritualized spectacle of a bullfight. In *The Sheltering Sky*, Paul Bowles obtains his essential simplification by an act of arbitrary violence, putting down a pair of New York sophisticates in the primitive Sahara. The act is precisely like the act of putting a smear of culture on a slide for inspection under the miscroscope.

Certainly no writer can see or know all or get all life into his fiction. His quality will be measured by the amount he does succeed in getting without blurring the edges of his simplifying frame. It is the frame, the limitation, that produces for the reader the limited field of vision that can be seen under an intense light and in sharpened focus.

The effect of reading fiction conceived and executed on such terms should be an enlarged understanding. But one element of this enlarged understanding which is too often overlooked is something I can call only "intense acquaintance." In all our wandering through real or fictional worlds it is probably ourselves we seek, and since that encounter is impossible we want the next-best thing: the completely intimate contact which may show us another like ourselves. I am willing if necessary to risk condemnation as an advocate of what C. S. Lewis has called the "personal heresy," though it is certainly no such biographical hunger as Mr. Lewis deplores that I speak of here. It is utterly irrelevant that Milton misused his daughters or that Conrad had a habit of flipping bread pellets around the dinner table. What is relevant is the artist himself, or his refined and distilled spirit, the totality of his understanding. Acquaintance on that level is a thing found very rarely in life, but a book which has profoundly and intensely moved us is a most intimate experience, perhaps more intimate than marriage and more revealing than fifty years of friendship. We can make closer contact in fiction than in reality; more surely than we know the secrets of our friends, we know how this writer who is something like ourselves looks upon himself, how he fronts his life, how he, another waif in a bewildering world, has made out to survive and perhaps be at peace.

Ultimately, I am convinced, he is what we read for. The work of art is not a gem, as some schools of criticism would insist, but truly a lens. We look through it for the purified and honestly offered spirit of the artist. The ghosts of meaning that flit past the windows of his fictional house wear his face. And the reward of a lifetime of reading is a rich acquaintanceship with those gentle or powerful or rebellious or acceptant, those greatly mixed and humanly various but always greatly human ghosts.

To a Young Writer

Your note asks advice on some purely practical matters, and to most of your questions the answers are dead-easy. No, you don't need any agent yet; later you probably will. Yes, you might try lifting sections out of your book and trying them on magazines; it can do no harm, and it might get you an audience or make you some money or both. No, there is no reason why you shouldn't apply for one of the available fellowships: Guggenheim or Saxton or, since you are uncommitted, one of those offered by publishers. By the same token, you are eligible to submit your book to any prize contest and to apply for admission to any of the literary and artistic colonies, such as Yaddo, the MacDowell Colony, or the Huntington Hartford Foundation. Even a brief residence in one of these would give you a place to live and write and would remove at least for a few weeks or months the insecurity that has nearly unnerved you. Of course I will write letters to any of these places in your behalf, of course I will give you letters to publishers, and if we happen to be in New York at the same time I will be happy to take you up to an office or two or three and introduce you.

But when I have said this, I am left feeling that most of what you really hoped to hear has been left unsaid. I suspect that much of the reason for your writing me was a need for reassurance: Your confidence had suddenly got gooseflesh and damp palms; you came up out of your book and looked around you and were hit by sudden panic. You would like to be told that you are good and that all this difficulty and struggle and frustration will give way gradually or suddenly, preferably suddenly, to security, fame, confidence, the conviction of having worked well and faithfully to a good end and become someone important to the world. If I am wrong in writing to this unspoken plea, forgive me; it is the sort of thing I felt myself at your age, and still feel, and will never get over feeling.

It is no trouble to tell you that you indeed are good, much too good to remain unpublished. Because publishers are mainly literate and intelligent, most of them are sure to see the quality in your novel, and one of them is sure to publish it. But that is as far as I can honestly go in reassurance, for I suspect he will publish it with little expectation of its making much money, either for him or for you.

Naturally I am not saying anything as foolish as that literary worth and popularity are incompatible. They are proved compatible quite frequently, but almost always when the writer in question possesses some form of the common touch—humor, sentiment, violence, sensationalism, sex, a capacity for alarm—and raises it to the level of art. Shakespeare and Rabelais and Mark Twain didn't exhaust the possibilities of lifting a whole mass of common preoccupations into beauty and significance. But it is your misfortune (and also your specific virtue) to have an uncommon touch. Your virtues are not the virtues of the mass of the population, or even of the reading population. Restraint, repose, compassion, humor that isn't ribald and feeling that isn't sentimental—these are caviar to the general, whatever you and I might wish.

You write better than hundreds of people with established literary reputations. You understand your characters and their implications, and you take the trouble to make sure that they have implications. Without cheating or bellowing or tearing a passion to tatters, you can bring a reader to that alert participation that is the truest proof of fiction's effectiveness. You think ten times where a lot of writers throb once.

And there is very little demand for the cool, perfect things you can do. You have gone threadbare for ten years to discover that your talents are almost sure to go unappreciated.

It is one thing to go threadbare for five or ten years in show business or to spend eight or ten years on a medical or legal education. A man can do it cheerfully, for the jackpots are there in those professions and may be expected by the talented in the course of time. And I suspect that you have had somewhere before you the marshlight of a jackpot, too. After all, every publishing season produces that happy sound of someone's apron being filled with solid, countable money. Your own seven years in college and two and a half years of apprenticeship on this first novel should entitle you to at least the milder sorts of expectation.

Since I participated in it, I know something about your education, and I know that it took. A literary education does not necessarily turn out even a good reader, much less a good writer. But with you it did both. You are a sharpened instrument, ready and willing to be put to work.

For one thing, you never took writing to mean self-expression, which means self-indulgence. You understood from the beginning that writing is done with words and sentences, and you spent hundreds of hours educating your ear, writing and rewriting and rewriting until you began to handle words in combination as naturally as one changes tones with the tongue and lips in whistling. I speak respectfully of this part of your education, because every year I see students who will not submit to it —who have only themselves to say and who are bent upon saying it without concessions to the English language. In acknowledging that the English language is a difficult instrument and that a person who sets out to use it expertly has no alternative but to learn it, you did something else. You forced yourself away from that obsession with self that is the strength of a very few writers and the weakness of so many. You have labored to put yourself in charge of your material; you have not fallen for the romantic fallacy that it is virtue to be driven by it. By submitting to language, you submitted to other disciplines, you learned distance and detachment, you learned how to avoid muddying a story with yourself.

That much the study of writing in college has given you. It might have given you worse things as well, but didn't. It might have made you a coterie writer, might have imprinted on you some borrowed style or some arrogance of literary snobbery, might have made you forever a leaner and a dependent. How many times have I backpedaled from some young man furious to destroy with words the father he thinks he hates; how many times have I turned cold to avoid becoming a surrogate father or even mother. How much compulsive writing have I read, inwardly flinching for the helpless enslavement it revealed. How often the writing of young writers is a way of asserting a personality that isn't yet there, that is only being ravenously hunted for.

None of that in yours. In yours, sanity and light and compassion, not self-love and self-pity. You know who you are, and you are good. Never doubt it—though you could not be blamed if you wistfully wondered. To date, from all your writing, you have made perhaps five hundred dollars, for two short stories and a travel article. To finance school and to write your novel you have lived meagerly with little encouragement and have risked the disapproval of your family, who have understandably said, "Here is this girl nearly thirty years old now, unmarried, without a job or a profession, still mooning away at her writing as if life were forever. Here goes her life through her fingers while she sits in cold rooms and grows stoop-shouldered over a typewriter." So now, with your book finally in hand, you want desperately to have some harvest: a few good reviews, some critical attention, encouragement, royalties enough to let you live and go on writing.

You are entitled to them all, but you may get few or none of them. Some good reviews you undoubtedly will get, but also many routine plus-minus ones that will destroy you with their impercipience, and a few flip ones by bright young men who will patronize you in five hundred words or spend their space telling how trying was the heat on the New Haven as they read this book on the commuters' special. Your initial royalty statement, at an optimistic guess, will indicate that your publisher by hard work built up an advance sale of 2,700 copies. Your next one, six months later, will probably carry the news that 432 of those copies came back and that altogether you fell just a little short of earning the thousand-dollar advance that you spent eight or nine months ago.

All this you are aware of as possibility, because you have the habit of not deceiving yourself and because you have seen it happen to friends. Learn to look upon it as probability.

Having brought yourself to that glum anticipation, ponder your choices. To go on writing as you have been doing—slowly, carefully, with long pauses for thinking and revising—you need some sort of subsidy: fellowship, advance, grant, job, marriage, something. In the nature of things, most of your alternatives will be both temporary and modest. Of the possible jobs, teaching probably offers most, because its hours are flexible and because it entails a three-month summer vacation. You have the training, the degrees, some teaching experience, but for you I would not advise teaching. For one thing, you are so conscientious that you would let it absorb your whole energy. For another, I am sure you can write only if you have full time for it. Your distillation process is slow, drop by drop, and you can't make it produce enough in a few broken weeks of summer. So you will undoubtedly try the fellowships and the colonies, and perhaps for a year or two get by that way.

After that, who knows? You might sell enough to squeak by; you might get a job caring for people's cats while they travel; you might work for a year or two at a time and save enough to take every third year for writing; you might marry. You might even marry and keep on writing, though it often happens otherwise. By the same token, you might find that marriage and children are so adequate a satisfaction of the urges that are driving you to write that you don't need to write, or you may find all the satisfactions of marriage and a family and come back to fiction when your children are grown. You and I both know those who have, and we both know some of the special difficulties they met. However you do it, I imagine you will always be pinched—for money, for time, for a place to work. But I think you will do it. And believe me, it is not a new problem. You are in good company.

Barring marriage, which is an alternative career and not a solution of this one, you may say to yourself that you can't stand
such a narrow, gray life, that you will modify your temperament and your taste, and work into your books some of the sensationalism, violence, shock, sentiment, sex, or Great Issues
that you think may make them attractive to a large audience. I
doubt that you could do it if you wanted to, and I am certain
that you shouldn't try, for you cannot write with a whole heart
things that are contrary to your nature. The fine things in your
first novel are there because you wrote them with a whole
heart, from an intense conviction. Trying to write like those
who manage a large popular success, you may succeed, because
you have brains and skill; but however proper success may be
for others, in you, and on these terms, it will not be legitimate,
for you will have stopped being the writer that you respected.

You are as whole an instrument as a broom. The brush is no
good without the handle, and the whole thing is good only for
sweeping. You are scheduled—doomed—to be a serious writer
regarding life seriously and reporting it to a small audience.
Other kinds of writers are both possible and necessary, but this
is the kind you are, and it is a good kind. Not many of your
countrymen will read you or know your name, not because they
are Americans, or moderns, or especially stupid, but because
they are human. Your kind of writer has never spoken to a
large audience except over a long stretch of time, and I would
not advise you to pin too much hope even on posterity. Your
touch is the uncommon touch; you will speak only to the
thoughtful reader. And more times than once you will ask yourself whether such readers really exist at all and why you should
go on projecting your words into silence like an old crazy actor
playing the part of himself to an empty theater.

The readers do exist. Jacques Barzun confidently guesses that
there are at least thirty thousand of them in the United States,
though they may have to be found vertically through many
years rather than horizontally in any one publishing season,
and though the hope of your reaching them all is about like the
possibility of your tracking down all the surviving elk in
America. But any of them you find you will treasure. This audi-

ence, by and large, will listen to what you say and not demand
that you say what everyone else is saying or what some fashionable school or clique says you should say. They are there, scattered through the apparently empty theater, listening and making very little noise. Be grateful for them. But however grateful
you are, never, never write to please them.

The moment you start consciously writing for an audience,
you begin wondering if you are saying what the audience wants
or expects. The peculiar virtue of this audience is that it leaves
up to you what should be said. You have heard Frank O'Connor speak of the difference between the private and the public
arts. Unless it is being dramatized or read aloud over the radio,
fiction is one of the private ones. The audience has nothing to
do with its making or with the slant it takes. You don't discover what should go into your novel by taking a poll or having
a trial run in Boston or Philadelphia. You discover it by thinking and feeling your way into a situation or having it feel its
way into you. From inside a web of relationships, from the very
heart of a temperament, your imagination creates outward and
forward.

You write to satisfy yourself and the inevitabilities of the situation you have started in motion. You write under a compulsion, it is true, but it is the compulsion of your situation, not of
a private hatred or envy or fear; and you write to satisfy yourself, but you write always in the remote awareness of a listener
—O'Connor's man in the armchair. He responds to what you
respond to and understands what you understand. Above all, he
listens. Being outside of you, he closes a circuit, he is an ear to
your mouth. Unless at least one like him reads you, you have
written uselessly. Your book is as hypothetical as the sound of
the tree that falls in the earless forest.

Nevertheless, I repeat, except for vaguely imagining him and
hoping he is there, ignore him, do not write what you think he
would like. Write what *you* like. When your book is published,
you will have a letter from at least one of him, perhaps from as
many as twenty or thirty of him. With luck, as other books
come on his numbers will grow. But to you he will always be a
solitary reader, an ear, not an audience. Literature speaks to

temperament, Conrad says. Your books will find the temperaments they can speak to.

And I would not blame you if you still asked, Why bother to make contact with kindred spirits you never see and may never hear from, who perhaps do not even exist except in your hopes? Why spend ten years in an apprenticeship to fiction only to discover that this society so little values what you do that it won't pay you a living wage for it?

Well, what goes on in your novel—the affectionate revelation of a relationship, the unraveling of the threads of love and interest binding a family together, the tranquil and not so tranquil emotions surrounding the death of a beloved and distinguished grandfather—this is closer to what happens in church than to what happens in the theater. Fiction always moves toward one or another of its poles, toward drama at one end or philosophy at the other. This book of yours is less entertainment than philosophical meditation presented in terms of personalities in action. It is serious, even sad; its colors and lights are autumnal. You have not loved Chekhov for nothing— maybe you imagined him as your reader in the armchair. He would listen while you told him the apparently simple thing you want to say: how love lasts, but changes, how life is full of heats and frustrations, causes and triumphs, and death is cool and quiet. It does not sound like much, summarized, and yet it embodies everything you believe about yourself and about human life and at least some aspects of the people you have most loved. In your novel, anguish and resignation are almost in balance. Your people live on the page and in the memory, because they have been loved and therefore have been richly imagined.

Your book is dramatized belief; and because in everyday life we make few contacts as intimate as this with another temperament and another mind, these scenes have an effect of cool shock—first almost embarrassment, then acknowledgment. Yes, I want to say. Yes, this is how it would be.

I like the sense of intimate knowing that your novel gives me. After all, what are any of us after but the conviction of belonging? What does more to stay us and keep our backbones stiff while the world reels than the sense that we are linked with someone who listens and understands and so in some way completes us? I have said somewhere else that the aesthetic experience is a conjugal act, like love. I profoundly believe it.

The worst thing that could happen to the ferocious seekers after identity is that they should find it and it only. There are many who do their best to escape it. Of our incorrigible and profound revulsion against identity, I suppose that physical love is the simplest, most immediate, and for many the only expression. Some have their comfort in feeling that they belong to the world of nature, big brother to the animals and cousin to the trees; some commit themselves to the kingdom of God. There is much in all of them, but for you, I imagine, not enough in any. For you it will have to be the kingdom of man, it will have to be art. You have nothing to gain and nothing to give except as you distill and purify ephemeral experience into quiet, searching, touching little stories like the one you have just finished, and so give your uncommon readers a chance to join you in the solidarity of pain and love and the vision of human possibility.

But isn't it enough? For lack of the full heart's desire, won't it serve?

The Writer and the Concept of Adulthood

If the term "adult" means anything, its meaning must be social. One does not declare oneself adult; one is perceived to be. Unavoidably, the qualities we call adult are on the side of "sanity," "normality," rationality, continuity, sobriety, responsibility, wisdom, conduct as opposed to mere behavior, the good of the family or group or species as distinct from the desires of the individual. It is unthinkable that we should call "adult" anyone who is unstable, extreme, or even idiosyncratic. In its purest form, adulthood is expressed in the characters of saints, sages, and culture heroes.

But in our pluralistic society, saints and sages are of many kinds, not always fully reconcilable. They derive from Christian, Jewish, Greek, and many other traditions. They have their roots in religion, law, humanistic ethics, art, in piety or skepticism, faith or stoicism or doubt, the agricultural or pastoral or industrial life, the tribe or the horde or the *civis*, wars or folkwanderings or myths. To those brought up in a tribal or ethnic or religious tradition which retains its integrity, the accepted saints and sages provide satisfying models of adulthood. A Hopi Indian knows, or used to know, pretty precisely what growing up to manhood or womanhood means. But if tradition is broken or unformed—if one is a black American, say—all guides may be unacceptable. To a black man who is fatherless, jobless, status-less, and without authority figures except those who have humiliated his race and him, the only attractive adult image may be that of avenger, an image of violence such as that once embraced by Eldridge Cleaver. And even so limited and essentially perverse a version of adulthood is subject to change as American society evolves. After another few centuries of the melting pot, one might expect a gradual reconciliation of our various notions of what it means to be grown up. On the other hand, if the present tendency toward accentuated ethnicity continues, there may never be a recognizably American adult, but instead the continuation and hardening of diverse and possibly hostile patterns within many subcultures.

One instrument of both preservation and change is obviously the artist, especially the writer. Even in an age of antiheroes and competing subcultures, he continues to create or report models for emulation or repudiation. Yet to examine the concept of adulthood as it relates to the concept of the artist—and to do it without an adequate definition of either—may seem an undertaking of dubious utility. For one thing, artists and writers are as various, and reflect as many competing traditions, as the rest of us. For another, artists are banned from the Republic and the company of the philosopher-kings precisely because, in their lives or their works or both, they are said not to demonstrate the sobriety and responsibility which the good of the state requires and which are basic to most of our tentative definitions of adulthood. Indeed, the Romantics from Blake and Wordsworth to D. H. Lawrence have insisted that the writer ought to be a child, or a primitive, and that acceptance of social obligations and duties, far from being a sign of maturity, is the saddest sort of surrender. Egocentrism, bohemianism, rebelliousness, lack of self-control and of that "developed strength" that Erik Erikson suspects is central to maturity—these are qualities we expect to find in writers and often do. We especially fear the artist in politics, but we rather fear him everywhere. He is an unsound man; and though he is a sort of anticoagulant in society, and hence indispensable, he has no clear social role. Not even the Internal Revenue Service allows for him on its forms. Not even our habit of nomenclature, which produces millions of Carpenters, Wheelwrights, Farmers, Fishers, Hunters, and Shepherds, has any family name such as Writer. The closest it comes is perhaps Clark, which is not the same thing by quite a margin.

The artist is as hard to define as the adult. There can be, and have been, Apollonian artists whose gifts of insight and wisdom ally them with that *vir* who is the vessel of *virtu*. But in our time the artist is likely to be Dionysian, marked not by the essentially conservative wisdom of the old chiefs but by the passion and recklessness of the young warriors. As he is generally perceived, and as he more often than not perceives himself, the writer has only the obligation to be open to experience, even to personally and socially destructive experience. He may even commit experience as fieldwork for his writing. He is the priest of human possibility, not of any limited system, and his fate is sometimes to be a sacrifice to his openness: sometimes we destroy him or ignore him to death because he threatens us, and later immortalize him because he has enlarged our vision. According to that pattern, Socrates was an "artist" done in by "adults." It is ironic that that interpretation was given to us by Plato, an artist who feared artists, an authoritarian adult uneasy about the coercive power of society.

Yet we should not, I think, dismiss artists from any consideration of adulthood. They are not quite gifted but irresponsible children; they are mixtures and approximations, like other concepts—like adults, for instance. And from the time of the invention of the alphabet, writers have themselves achieved status as saints and sages. Moreover, writers are not static. They grow and change, and perhaps they grow toward greater wisdom and responsibility; perhaps there are stages in their lives that correspond to the stages of childhood, adolescence, adulthood, and senility in the life of Everyman. Perhaps, furthermore, the very qualities that self-protective societies find dangerous are the proofs of a higher adulthood, beyond and above the prescriptive and limited adulthood that limited societies feel comfortable with. Writers would like to think so. "What is Chaos?" asks Stanisław Lec. "It is the Order destroyed during Creation."

There are writers of every stature. We are talking, I presume, only about the serious and gifted. And I have never known a serious writer who wasn't as responsible, in his way, as any priest or professor or public servant. The difference is that a writer is responsible not to a tradition or a church or any sort of social stability and conformity, but to his personal vision of truth and social justice, to his gift. That often sets him at odds with the "adults" of his system, but it also makes him indispensable. His vision and the integrity with which he pursues and promotes it are elements needed for a larger and more humane synthesis, which in the nature of things will again harden and will need once more the services of iconoclasts.

Iconoclasts, moreover, who *work*—whose work is never done, whose work is coterminous with consciousness and energy, who are diligent, self-disciplined, independent, and endlessly patient. Work is the means through which a writer puts into communicable and evocative and perhaps memorable form what he wants to say. If any quality seems to entitle him to be called adult, it is his capacity for work. Unfortunately, this society's attitudes toward work are so ambiguous that they call for some preliminary discussion.

There is hardly an activity of man so consistently bad-mouthed as work. It has had a hostile press since Genesis 3:19. Children are warned that all work and no play makes Jack a dull boy. At least in some moods, we associate work with discomfort, imprisonment, fatigue, boredom, indignity, exploitation, everything that hangs like chains around the ankles of our pleasures. Those who affect to like work, we call victims of the puritan work ethic; we tell them that if they don't relax and let the pleasure principle in, they will suffer consequences compared to which cholera would seem benign.

Work is what almost everybody says he would rather be doing anything else than. Fantasies of work's unpleasantness are matched by counterfantasies of idyllic laziness and liberation. In keeping with some Huckleberry Finn wishfulness that inhabits our mental cupboards next to memories of Poor Richard, a hundred million non-fishing American men, asked what they would do if work were abolished tomorrow, reply that they would find a grassy bank, lay in a good supply of beer, and lie down with a fishline tied around their toe to watch a cork bob in lazy water forever.

We all partially subscribe to the stereotype that puts work and pleasure at opposite ends of the scale. Children, who do not have to work, are envied by adults, who do. Five days, the script goes, we grudgingly labor, and on the sixth and seventh we renew ourselves. Vacations are all that keep us from being pulverized by the old grind. We work at our recreation very hard, and when we limp exhausted back to factory or office we are greeted by groans of sardonic sympathy. Back to the salt mines, ha ha. Hello, sucker.

Thus the folklore of industrial and corporate man. Recovery from work is the excuse for many diversions, from managerial alcoholism and call girls to blue-collar taverns with topless waitresses and Saturday-night brawls. Yet most of us, even those of us who work at routine jobs, don't dislike work as much as we say we do. Not too rebelliously, we accept the fact that work is what we build our lives around, and many of us discover it to be a satisfaction, even a pleasure. It not only gets us what we need and want, it proves to us that we are grown up.

We are at least as industrious a species as the ants, even while we disparage the work ethic. If our play is sometimes work, so is our work sometimes play. We think we get more fun out of life than the people we vaguely call puritans. But nobody ever accused Ben Franklin of being dour, even if he did write *Poor Richard's Almanack*; and who is to say that John Cotton, rising at three to study Greek and Hebrew Scriptures for three hours before his day's work properly began, and closing out his eighteen-hour workday by sweetening his mouth with a bit of Calvin before sleeping, was not enjoying himself? Joy in work is largely a matter of motivation, and Cotton's urge to walk piously with God was perhaps as effective a motivation as that of Dr. Freud, another man who worked himself very hard.

Even parents who habitually pursue the pleasure principle from Las Vegas to Puerto Vallarta may have a disconcerting and not entirely consistent way of urging, driving, and bribing their children to work hard in school. When children become adolescents, moreover, and begin to yearn for the independence and presumed freedom of adulthood, few, even in these days of the counterculture, question the law that ties their maturity to self-supporting labor. As it said on the gate at Auschwitz, *Arbeit macht frei*. And pleasure-prone American parents are likely to consider their child's first serious job a rite of passage comparable to graduation from high school. The fathers of the sixteen-year-old boys I sometimes hire as handymen consult me anxiously in private: How's the kid doing? Has he learned to work? Can he do a job?

If he has, if he can, he has begun to "grow up." Work is perhaps the ultimate measure of adulthood. Pleasure in work is another and more debatable matter, for even those who accept work willingly may pretend to dislike it. Yet the pleasure principle, which is supposedly incompatible with work, has a way of entering quietly by the employees' entrance. Many an individual finds, on retirement, that during his life he has got more fun out of his work than out of his fun. Thrown into total leisure and unproductiveness, he invents jobs in order to have them to do. The companionship of fellow workers and the satisfactions of a shared function turn out to be more valuable than we ever thought while we had them. That goes for workers whose jobs have been routine as well as for those who have enjoyed a certain professional autonomy. As the retired executive may yearn for the sense of power and usefulness that his desk once gave him, the ex-postman's feet wistfully remember the comfortable turnings and re-turnings of his old route.

In short, more people than would probably admit it find in work the scaffolding that holds up the adult life. Of course it can be a compulsion, a neurotic symptom: Like almost any human activity, it can be carried to that excess that constitutes sin. But even when it is compulsive and neurotic it may be the only thing that holds a life together; for what is a neurosis but an adaptation, designed to keep disintegration and panic at arm's length? And sometimes work is more than a satisfaction, a comfort, a habit, or a sanctuary. It is a joy.

Levin reaping his fields with a crowd of peasants in *Anna Karenina* is exalted beyond thought or fatigue. His anxious self-questioning is lulled, his sensuous perceptions are heightened by the delight of rhythmical muscular exercise and by associa-tion with men whose physical competence is a challenge and whose integrity as workmen he respects. I have seen executives on vacation, playing at bringing in wood from a woodlot, expe-rience the same intense pleasure. I have experienced it myself with a crew of Vermont farmers cooperating around a drag saw. Women preparing a church supper, students organizing a bonfire or a confrontation, even a detail of soldiers digging a la-trine will experience it if health and morale are good. I suppose some optimum of work-pleasure is achieved by a string quartet either practicing or performing. The joy of joint effort is at the heart of all team sports. Alexis de Tocqueville, observing quilt-ing and husking bees and neighborhood barn raisings, thought their communal labor one of the most attractive as well as one of the most democratic aspects of American life. In an odd way, moreover, this shared work that effaces the individual also enhances him. Even more than competition, it makes him do his best, and better than his best.

[I should say so!]

Unfortunately communal work-joy is incompatible with in-dustrial capitalism, so that our feelings about it are mixed. It is too easily exploited. It weakens the hand of collective bargain-ing. Also, it has bad political associations. Dictators both left and right are students of the symbols, slogans, songs, parades, and eurhythmics that help produce this productive form of group hysteria. When we heard from travelers that China was full of smiling people in blue blouses happily carrying out the directives of Chairman Mao, we asked why we heard of no such unanimity among artists and intellectuals, why the cul-tural revolution was thought necessary. We answered ourselves with the assurance that Mao had the same view of artists that

Plato did. Artists and intellectuals don't relish the role of Pavlov's dog or the worker bee. They are unsound, dangerous to the system, and hence (it could be argued) un-adult.

So communal work-joy does not seem to have much of a future in America, outside the activities of musical groups, sports teams, certain academic and research organizations, and spontaneous associations of farmers, vacationers, and eleemosynary volunteers. Our aspiration is in the opposite direction, toward maximum self-realization as individuals. When Edwin Land, the founder and president of the Polaroid Corporation, tells us that the worker is entitled to more than an eight-hour day with two martinis at the end, the "more" that he has in mind is not Chinese enthusiasm and unanimity, but the individual pleasures of creativity and problem-solving. When Mr. Land himself is on a problem he is at the lab at all hours of the day and night, because nothing else he could be doing could possibly interest him so much or give him so much pleasure. He would like to give all workers a chance at the sort of work-pleasure he himself enjoys. When we come down to it, that isn't greatly different, except in its objectives, from the dedicated strenuousness of a John Cotton.

Work folklore to the contrary notwithstanding, that is what many kinds of Americans hunger for. They try to evade or supplant the system, not cooperate with it. The young people who flee industrial civilization and build their log cabins, yurts, or geodesic domes in the woods, there to live off their subsistence gardens while their children grow up as a part of the wildlife, are following a fad, certainly, and repeating the perennial American fantasy of a return to innocence, and sometimes paradoxically submerging themselves in an alternative group. But they are not running from work. They are only trying to restore to work the elective freedom, the meaningfulness and joy, that industrialism has taken out of it. Instead of tightening individual nuts, they want to handle the whole product. They want to pursue their own ends, not those of a corporation. They prefer the human (sometimes the tribal) to the industrial scale. Neither the collectively bargained-for reluctance of the assembly line nor the singing unison of the hive satisfies them.

Significantly, a lot of them yearn to be artists or writers or craftsmen; they take up leatherworking or wood sculpture or blacksmithing, they make miles of macramé. Papered-over puritans, they aspire to a working autonomy that in our society is now enjoyed principally by experimental scientists, intellectuals on fellowships, hermits, free craftsmen, and hippies with trust funds. The artist's relation to his work—autonomous, independent, creative, free, joyful, and presumably easy because uncoerced—is the relation many of us entangled in the world's drudgery yearn toward. We pay our writers the compliment of envy and emulation, even while, as a society, we disparage their easy and irresponsible life, or try to sterilize them with celebrity.

I suppose that creation—the creation, say, of a novel—is one of the highest pleasures available to us, pleasure at a godlike level. But the novelist's life is not quite the carefree matter that popular condescension and envy assume. As De Lawd said in *The Green Pastures,* "Bein' God ain't no bed of roses." The more independent work is, the more solitary it is likely to be. It rarely involves enough of the stimulation of human warmth and contact. Its sharing is more often done after the fact than during the act. It breeds no songs, chanteys, dances, or any of the spontaneous folklore which, once created, adds enthusiasm and delight to the work it sprang from. Writers, especially, often work with an austerity that is close to puritan, and with a dedication that approaches, and often becomes, compulsion.

The self-starting, self-directed, self-disciplined writer is commonly a harsher boss to himself than any external boss could be. He is his own victim. Unlike a compulsive moneymaker or tycoon, he cannot at a certain age divest himself of his monomania and turn his life to enjoyment of his gains by becoming a gourmand or a collector of paintings. He can no more be relieved of his creative curse than Hawthorne's Georgiana could be relieved of her birthmark.

It is entangled with the very roots of his life. Hundreds of writers, ancient and modern, have testified that a day without work is a day lost, and some of the saddest people in the long sad history of mankind have been creators whose creativity wore out before they did. One such, as his *Life in Letters* makes clear, was John Steinbeck. In considering the ways in which a writer's life may be given its shape and meaning by his management of or by his gift, I have Steinbeck frequently in mind.

It is all but standard for serious writers to coerce their creative activity into a frame of habit. Except for amateurs and dilettantes, writing is not a part-time occupation, nor is it the automatic spilling over of genius. It is the hardest kind of work, the making of something from nothing. No one but a dedicated, disciplined, even bullheaded individual is going to go on, day after day, sweating for five or six hours to make a page that may have to be thrown away tomorrow. If, as Henry Adams said, chaos is the law of nature and order the dream of man, and if the imposition of order on a corner of chaos is the function—or the illusion—of art, then the writer feels obliged to begin by imposing order on himself, at least during working hours. "The getting to work is a purely mechanical thing, as you well know—a conscious and self-imposed schoolroom," Steinbeck wrote to a friend. "After that, other things happen, but the beginning is straight pushing."

The establishment of a working routine is more than a means of making oneself toe the line. It is also a protection from interruption by friends, acquaintances, and strangers who assume that since you are at home you are not working, and who further assume that even if you are, your work is like other work and may be lightened and sweetened by interruption. The writer at work is submerged, and every intrusion that draws him to the surface costs him his concentration. More than that, his routine is part of a mystique. His time is braced on every side by habits and propitiations. The writing is not only done during certain regular hours, it is likely to involve a foreplay as essential as that of sex. We sharpen pencils, clear the desk, change the ribbon, warm up the fingers by writing a letter or two. We fritter and putter, we read over yesterday's pages and perhaps rewrite them, perhaps throw them away. We work closer and closer, not being too obvious about where we are headed, until all at once we are there, and writing. That is when we need a wife who will answer the telephone or the doorbell and swear we are not at home. As a matter of fact, we're not.

Furthermore, no writer I ever knew wants to examine too closely what goes on when he is writing well. (I exempt Arthur Koestler, who had already given up writing novels before he took up the study of creativity.) I have seen a pair of distinguished psychologists meet only stony suspicion and refusal when they asked members of my advanced fiction seminar to volunteer as hypnotic subjects. The idea was to sneak up on their creativity when it wasn't looking. Those young writers did not want their creativity sneaked up on. They felt it to be not only intensely personal, but fragile. Instead of exposing or analyzing it, they surrounded it with a camouflage of routine and casualness. They kept it in its hideout, where it was safe; only at *their* will, not at that of some investigator, did they turn it loose to make its raids on human experience.

Ordinarily, the establishment of working habits goes on simultaneously with a writer's exploration of his talent, discovery of his themes and subject matters, and finding and polishing of techniques. The habit of work is perfected in a time of promise, ambition, hope, and often crazy energy. It is a time of great happiness for many, for they are both discovering themselves and putting themselves to use. They are exemplars of the examined life; and their examination is not isolated and analytic, but synthetic and in context. They are constructing, in stories, novels, poems, or plays, scale models of their insights and beliefs. They know the joy of creating a world.

Many writers, perhaps most, have found their workrooms places of sanctuary, and work a magic that exorcises demons. "By God, I envy you people," a psychologist told me once. "You can write your lives instead of having to live them." He was not quite accurate. One does both, and simultaneously. I helped my mother die, and I was writing with some part of my mind much of the time. When I received word of my father's death, I said, without premeditation and to my own dismay, "Now I know how that novel ends." The writing habit can be a carefully prepared schizophrenic closet into which one retires to make intolerable reality into something bearable.

Such experiences mark the first and most exhilarating stage of the characteristic novelist's career. The second has arrived when subject matters and themes have been found, techniques learned, audience achieved. It is not a stage that happens to everyone. Fledgling writers make it to safety about as infrequently as newly hatched turtles or salmon fry. But for those who do, this is the stage of self-confident achievement, emancipated from too much self-scrutiny.

So what was at first spontaneous, absorbing, full of discovery and delight is disciplined into a habit rich in satisfactions, and then becomes a refuge whose pleasures are more rueful, to be accepted with gratitude. And if personal troubles threaten to get out of hand, or if new themes come harder or not at all, if creation comes hard, or stops entirely, then there is a third stage, marked by desperation and compulsion. Instead of enjoying his work habit, or finding safety in it, the writer may become imprisoned in it, and work may become a self-made hell. Like a dwindling oil well, the novelist has to pump ever harder for what little he produces. Or like a beaver whose teeth grow constantly, he must chew incessantly, not to eat, not to build dams, but simply to keep his jaws from being locked shut.

There is such a thing as writer's block, there is such a thing as being written out. A writer who lasts through several decades can hardly avoid experiencing both in some degree. I remember Walter D. Edmonds, once a dazzling success story among the writers of Cambridge, Mass. About 1941 he ran into a total block. The harder he tried, the less anything worked. He never succeeded in writing again, except for children, but I know he went through all the circles of hell clear to the ninth, which, as if to accommodate writers, is lonely and cold, before he adjusted himself to silence. I remember Bernard DeVoto after he had written the trilogy of Western histories which were so clearly what he had been born to write; he suddenly found himself without book. Art, he had said, was man determined to die sane. Art was the instrument and proof of self-control. For a long time he carried on the professional hackwork and the essays on public affairs that he had always done as a second full-time job. They didn't satisfy. The desk which had been both a sanctuary and the place of deepest satisfaction became a prison and an excuse. The creative excitement dried off like mist off a windowpane and let him look through to what he didn't want to see. The compulsive worker who for years had held off dread and panic could no longer hold them off, and he died desperate.

Happiness in work? Satisfaction in work? I know they exist, for I have experienced them. But I am sobered by the many writers who in order to pacify their demon turned work into a compulsive habit and found themselves at the end enclosed in it, as empty as the shell of a dead tortoise. What does the novelist do when the awareness that this has happened comes in on him? Sometimes he works all the harder, a machine that at least for the time being cannot do anything but run. Often he projects great plans to persuade himself of something: that this will be the biggest thing in his whole career. Eventually he might have to admit that he is "written out." One of the special anguishes of a writer in this condition is the fact that writers, by definition and profession, are *aware*. Often they also have an overdeveloped sense of mission. It is very hard to accept the end of their specialness.

And what does this tell us about adulthood? Nothing very coherent, I fear. It raises more questions than it provides answers. Is the novelist, threatening as he often is to our conventions and assumptions and socially protective inhibitions, dangerous child or prophet? Was Steinbeck, for example—exposing the exploitation and social injustices of California's factories in the fields—the hateful radical the growers thought him or the prophet he seemed to Americans with a developed social conscience? I suppose he was both, for the growers had to move over and make room for reforms that *The Grapes of Wrath* made inevitable. By his choice of subject matter and the direction of his sympathies and the expression of his anger, he established himself as a milestone on the road to César Chavez and the United Farm Workers of America, and so as a kind of

champion of social justice. By speaking from within the democratic mass, he offended the literary intellectuals, who
dismissed, and still dismiss, his work as middlebrow. Where
does adulthood lie among such contradictions?

There are other questions raised by the decline of a writer's
creative powers. Is adulthood only a stage, the stage of full
vigor and confidence, in the life of a writer? Is an author
"adult" only during his middle years, when he is full of things
to say, has developed the means to say them, and perhaps has a
vast audience to say them to? Does his growing anxiety and
eventual silence represent a decline from adulthood, a diminish-
ment toward impotence and senility, or should we take them as
a maturing into sad but acceptant wisdom, a fully matured
stage when personal desires, ambition, and the other vanities
have been worn out and the writer's mind is clear, passionless,
only faintly regretful? How much does personal serenity, that
state so seldom observed among men and women of any profession, define adulthood?

I do not know, for our notions of adulthood are various and
contradictory, but I do know that many writers display those
ambiguous symptoms and suggest the same questions. Was the
Sinclair Lewis of *Main Street* and *Babbitt*, during the years
when he was in full vigor and capable of the most acid commentary on mid-American life, more or less mature than the
chastened Sinclair Lewis of *It Can't Happen Here* and *The
Prodigal Parents*, books whose theme was the unspectacular
but utterly essential goodnesses and stabilities of middle-class
life threatened by fascism or by youthful intransigence? Young
warriors do sometimes become old chiefs, even among artists.
They seem to go through stages like the rest of us, and at various stages they embody and celebrate various aspects of our social aspiration, differing versions of good. What may begin as a
determination to remake the world in the image of perfection,
or express only its highest ideals or its most civilized aspects,
may subside into the tired perception that the ideal is an impossible dream and that the best anyone can do is to help hold
things together with sticking plaster. Is it more "adult" to
aspire to the impossible or to accept imperfection?

Moreover, the stages that sometimes seem to be apparent in the lives and works of writers may be less precise than they appear to be. The fact is that literature is helplessly culture-bound, which means that in a pluralistic society it reflects the wildest variety of norms, and that variety itself changes with time, with the changing proportions and dominances among the populations, and much else. As the mordant Stanisław Lec remarks, every stink that fights the ventilator thinks it is Don Quixote. But it does not follow that every such stink can be ignored. Sometimes it *is* Don Quixote. Not every child who plays with fire can be ignored either. Sometimes he turns out to be Prometheus. So it is impossible to say that youthful rebellion against law, convention, custom, and prevailing literary practice is necessarily immature and that more conservative responses are more adult.

We grow up unevenly, into a world which puts uneven values on our qualities. By a kind of consensus, the dedication and self-discipline that artists quite commonly display in their work entitle them to be called, at least in that respect, mature. But what is written in those disciplined hours may be absurd, jejune, unreal, dead wrong. Work discipline may serve illusion and self-deception and, occasionally (at least in the view of some readers), downright evil. On the other hand, if adulthood is held to be the hard-won product of age, thought, and experience, it is almost inevitably allied with resignation, and its strongest counsel will be caution. Nestor, not Odysseus and certainly not either Achilles or Agamemnon, becomes the adult model—and we have no counsel which could lead either to the fighting or the writing of the Trojan War, a testing ground for heroes.

We grow up unevenly. It is unlikely that we will see, among writers or among the population at large, any individual who is clearly and unambiguously culture hero, saint, or sage. What we are more likely to find is that collection of contradictory qualities, that *homme moyen sensuel,* whom by a process of averaging we agree to call adult. He will have in him some element of the man who sets out to change what he cannot bear and some element of the man who makes up his mind to bear what he cannot change. He may be wise, he may in fact be a true sage, as Robert Frost was one; yet, along with his profundity and wisdom, Frost displayed both in private and in public an unbecoming malice, and he was given to childish tantrums. Or he may be strictly controlled and disciplined, as in his writing Ernest Hemingway was, and never grow up beyond envy and spite, never write a line, however disciplined, that is uncorrupted by his own egomania.

I do not believe that adulthood is definable as a stage in the life either of artists or of less-self-conscious mortals. I do not believe that it is even a precise cluster of qualities, for qualities differ depending on the point of view and the time and the circumstances. Adulthood, I should say, is always an approximation—a failed approximation. Among the saints it may be justified by faith; more generally it is shaped by indecision and doubt. And I think it does not necessarily last from the time when it is approximately achieved to the time when the coffin lid is closed upon the serene and upward-staring face. It is a stage on the way to senility—or, in the case of many writers, a tentative, half-scared, half-hopeful, nearly compulsive time for the exploitation of a gift that at any time may be cruelly withdrawn.

Excellence and the Pleasure Principle

Let me say at once that I am here not as an expert qualified to solve problems, but as a bewildered pilgrim. Chekhov said it wasn't a writer's job to solve problems; his job was only to state them correctly. And even there I feel deficient.

The fact is, I can't tell you what pleasure is, or how many kinds there are, or whether some kinds are worthier than others, or what the principle of pleasure is, if any. Or what excellence is, or how achieved. Or whether the pursuit of pleasure and the pursuit of excellence are compatible or incompatible goals.

I don't know whether this consumer-oriented, desire-stimulating, resource-devouring society we have created is the predictable achievement of American progress, mankind's rosy fulfilled dream, or whether it is the red sunset of Götterdämmerung. We find much wrong with our society, but most of us, in the pinch, would choose it over any alternative the world offers, because without any question it is the freest as well as one of the most comfortable. We sell it eagerly to others, even while growing numbers get frozen out of it, or get sick of it, or drop out of it, at home. We take it for granted that the "de-

veloping" nations will be better off when they have pulled themselves "up" to our industrially organized, gratification-happy,
pollution-blackened system—and so, in fact, do they. A lot of
anti-Americanism in the world is pure envy.

We cheer the entry of Pepsi into Russia and Coke into
China: thin edge of the wedge, the first sliding coil of our be-
guiling serpent into those Communist Edens. But at the same
time, the mountains of Idaho and Montana and the woods of
Vermont fill up with thousands of mainly young people in
flight from our American blessings. They live, by singles and
couples and communes, in yurts and geodesic domes and ret-
rofitted chicken houses, own no TV sets, wear muumuus and
patched jeans, go barefoot, exalt manual labor as the most *in*
form of pleasure, cherish hardship, discomfort, independence,
and irresponsibility about equally, and subsist on organic vegetables, trust funds, and food stamps.

Is this utopia or dystopia, an optimistic repetition of new beginnings or disillusion, revolution or devolution or simply volu-
tion. I don't know.

As a society, we are a bundle of contradictions, conflicts,
fragmentations, colliding moralities, and changes so swift and
constant that we come closer than any civilization in history to
being experimental. We don't have a national life, we have life-
styles, all kinds of life-styles, in a constant flux that may be
working up to perfection by a series of regular steps and may,
on the other hand, be pointlessly circular.

Is it, for example, emancipation or demoralization when
many of us substitute what a poet friend of mine calls "free-
form" marriage for the old, monogamous kind? Depends on
who you are. But if it is emancipation, a breakthrough, why is
divorce such a tearing trauma for so many, and why is a whole
area of sociology concerned with the problems of children
adrift in broken or reconstituted homes? Is the sexual revolution a way to equality for women, and a path into new freedom, health, beauty, and emotional satisfaction, as advertised,
or is it a return to the abominations that got Sodom and
Gomorrah a bad press and brought on the Flood? Depends on
who you are. Every pleasure is ultimately a collaboration or a

conflict—it intersects somewhere with the interests of others, or with the public interest, as when motorcycle rallies, which are probably fun for the participants, destroy whole areas of fragile desert. As for the pleasures of the flesh, do we listen to the swingers or the psalm singers? If we go with the swingers as more exciting and new, how far do we go with them? Do we stop at what Mailer calls the minor drugs, or press forward? Do we content ourselves with the sorts of pleasures suggested by *Oui* and *Penthouse* and the tamer skin flicks, or do we explore all the universes of hard porn, where what used to be called perversions are as commonplace as dandruff, and sex is the only, and the kinkiest, game in town? If we like this investigation of the sensuous and the celebration/exploitation of the body's twitches, do we limit the contestants to consenting adults, or do we proceed into the more exotic operations: captives, children, defectives, monsters, animals, snuff movies? If we feel these new pleasures are psychologically good for us, and by grace of antibiotics and the pill harm no one, then what do we do about the multiplication of sex crimes and the escalating VD and illegitimacy rates and the sexual exploitation of children? There are always sour puritans to suggest that this sort of emancipation is actually imprisonment, obsession; that we have broken down inhibitions to achieve disorder; that we have come out of inertia into St. Vitus's dance.

We are a nation of highly stimulated appetites. Some of our most serious domestic problems derive from the stimulation of appetites for things—everything that the Constitution promises and everything the movies and television and magazines and the shop windows display—without providing the economic or other means of gratifying them. But even when we are born lucky, or achieve luck, or have luck thrust upon us, and are able to have all these goodies, there may be a hollowness in the pit of our souls. In medieval terms, our besetting deadly sins are lust and gluttony: As a nation we are oversexed and overweight. In our Belshazzar's feast, some of us may have read the handwriting on the wall—and some of us have heard the voice of Goethe commenting on Faust and those like him who strive always for fulfillment and in fulfillment strain to feel desire.

How pleasurable are the pleasures we value, and how lasting? What alternatives do we have for them? Is there any escape from them? Is it perhaps time for some prophet to come out of the hills with foxtails in his beard and a scourge of star thistles in his hand, crying, Woe, woe unto this people? Have we begun to crave the sackcloth and self-humiliation of a spiritual rebirth? The number of cults we generate suggests that a lot of us have. Unhappily, the prophets are generally entrepreneurs in the best American tradition—and shortly are seen driving Rolls Silver Streaks in the company of Las Vegas-type blondes and, on the occasion of their investigation by a grand jury, are found to have bank accounts in six countries.

Should we try to reverse the engines? Do we need to return to plain living and high thinking and turn away from Roman decadence? Are there other, less hedonistic, more lasting pleasures that could be made as available as we now make the physical ones? Or is what the psalm singers call decadence a final shaking off of Victorian trammels, an emergence into a brave new world where we can enjoy the excesses of our liberty and the overabundance of our pleasures without guilt feelings? I don't know.

One thing I do know. It is unsafe to speak of anything American, including American pleasure, as if it were something single, unified, and unanimous. A few years ago, living in Canada, I was astonished to find that some Canadians look upon us as a single, definable, obnoxious thing, the big hateful monolith that keeps Canada a branch-plant economy, the homogenized mass culture that overwhelms all Canadian difference, all Canadian excellence.

We are so far from being a monolith that sometimes I wonder if one could find ten Americans who think alike. One nation, under God, indivisible, the pledge of allegiance says. But under what God? And some Americans won't take the pledge. We have approached unity only twice in our national life, during the crises of two world wars, and that unity was far from complete. The melting pot that was supposed to boil us down into comfortable conformity has spectacularly failed to do so. The Civil War that we fought to reunite the Union didn't. Not even the mass media that some accuse of homogenizing us have succeeded in making a *unum* out of our *pluribus*. We retain, or develop, stubborn ethnic, religious, and regional identities. Our bloods and loyalties and colors are of the wildest variety. We are not the white Protestant nation of Northern European origin that we started out to be. We are by no means entirely a Christian nation, and our recent religious life-styles have been more African and Asian than European. Politically we are everything from neo-Nazis to Zen meditators. Despite Cronkite, Lawrence Welk, and "I Love Lucy," an Oregonian can be distinguished from an Alabaman, and a native of Santa Fe is another creature from one who has lived his life in the Bronx.

Region is actually a more potent divider than economic class —perhaps as potent as color and creed. A white banker from Atlanta probably has as much in common with a black Georgia sharecropper as he does with another white banker from Salt Lake City or Seattle. And there is always age, the celebrated generation gap, if other divisions fail. People born on the far side of World War II, no matter what their color, creed, region, or economic class, are another people from those born on the near side. A lot of assumptions were at least temporarily blown up by Vietnam, civil rights, women's liberation, and the pill.

But over all of this variety, over young and old, just and unjust, rich and poor, shines the pale sunshine of the pleasure-loving state of mind. Pleasure is the aim and end of the popular culture; appetites and their satisfaction are a theme with endless variations, a business with enormous resources and persuasiveness. The tune pleases some less than others, but it reaches us all. In California especially, new country without marked provincial or regional character, young people's country, outdoor country, sport country, fun country, peach bowl, experimental society, without history, adrift in the present, addicted to Now and Wow—America, only more so—pleasure is the denominator, almost the criterion by which we judge good and bad. The popular heroes and heroines, the only heroes some acknowledge, are sports figures, or movie-TV celebrities— entertainers. In California we no longer say, "Good-bye—God be wi' ye." We say, "Have a good day. Have fun."

And that brings me, by a long, epicycloidal route, to what I want to talk about: the compatibility between the search for excellence and the pursuit of pleasure. Because you are who you are and I am who I am, I want to talk about it in the terms suggested by the profession of teaching and the profession of letters.

Again I must be very tentative. Though I was a teacher for more than forty years and have been a writer for nearly fifty, and have sat on the other end of a log from many a schoolboy and schoolgirl, and have set up my mirror in the roadway and watched change go by, I don't pretend to know what is the duty of either a teacher or a writer in these times. I assume that both of us have something to do with instruction, something to do with entertainment. But the emphasis and the proportions are negotiable, and both of us are often charged with failure on both counts.

It is commonly charged against teachers that Johnny can't read—or write, or add without his fingers or a calculator, or find his way in the library door, or use a dictionary. A frequent suggestion is that teacher must work harder to motivate Johnny, the assumption being that if teacher doesn't make the class as entertaining as an X-rated movie, teacher is muffing the job.

From what I have seen of students and teachers, I think it quite as likely that Johnny is muffing the job; and that he is muffing it not because he is more stupid than he used to be but because he is less teachable; and that he is less teachable because something in his family, or his society, or himself, has broken down. The authority, parental or otherwise, that once made Johnny respect the hard process of stocking and exercising his mind, has been softened up and worn away, in considerable part by Johnny himself. Now Johnny makes up his own mind, or thinks he does, about what is important to him. Actually, what makes up his mind is the movies, television, and advertising, all the incessant repetitions of the mass media and the easy assumptions of popular culture. They tell him that book learning is a pain and a bore. He likes better to look at pictures than to work out the difficult symbolic system of print, and he looks at the easiest pictures. Years ago, when I worked for a while for *Look* magazine, it used to be a staff joke that *Look* was made for those too dumb to understand the pictures in *Life*. *Look* helped make things easy for Johnny, as some early Johnnies had helped make *Look*.

Johnny's due and destiny, as the popular culture reads them to him, are satisfaction of desires, acquisition of things, gratification, stereos, dune buggies, ORV's, trail bikes, laughing beautiful companions, rock, intimate whispers, fun: either that or envy of those who have these things. Johnny is a citizen of the world village that Marshall McLuhan wrote of. His world is oral, not printed; pictorial or musical, not verbal; immediate, not grounded in history; impromptu, not planned; experienced, not examined; free, not disciplined. To those who shoot down on the schools from protected places, I would suggest a possibility: that Johnny has been spoiled rotten by something entirely outside the formal educational process and beyond formal educational cure.

I don't have to tell this audience that when education is both universal and compulsory; when it has to make an impossible equation between the democratic IQ and intellectual excellence; when a certain proportion of its students are close to ineducable either because of low intelligence, poor background, color disadvantage, lack of interest, or some specific handicap such as dyslexia; when Proposition 13 and other disasters to the budget make individual teaching, special programs, remedial reading, and other things impossible; when parents with a less than objective view of their children's capacity challenge both methods and grades; when large classes, heavy teaching schedules, and a load of administrative, counseling, and PTA duties put such burdens on an English teacher that the assignment of a single theme is an act of heroism or foolhardiness—when conditions such as these obtain, the system is not going to be able to reach out and correct the ills of the society at large, and shouldn't be asked to.

I have never taught in high school, but I think I understand a little of how it goes. And when to the rest of the handicaps are added racial tensions, public criticism, public indifference, and the falling away of public respect for teachers, I don't wonder that people are leaving the profession to drive taxis or sell real estate. I wish they wouldn't, but I understand why they do.

Furthermore, like everything else in this country, the reports on Johnny are contradictory. At the same time that we hear he can't read, we hear from other loudspeakers that Johnny is miles ahead of where his grandparents and parents were at the same age. He is better informed, better trained to think, more confident, more committed. I have seen plenty of both kinds of Johnny, and I have to believe that both reports are true as observed fact, but misleading as generalizations. I suspect that good students are better than they ever were. I also suspect that bad students are worse, not only because they are less amenable to instruction but because the forms of instruction, which used to stress the memorization and repetition most useful to the dull or dyslectic, now stress the creative thinking most stimulating to the gifted; and finally, because the bigger and more bureaucratic the educational system becomes, the harder it is for really exciting teaching to take place.

But if there has been a decline in the effectiveness of primary and secondary teaching, it is a statistical decline, not a collapse. We can take comfort from the fact that no matter how bad a system is, it can't spoil a good student.

All sorts of Americans in ruder times got an education with bad teachers or no teachers at all. They spread themselves like sheets of flypaper to catch every particle of knowledge. They made themselves into the kind upon whom nothing is lost. They coveted excellence; excellence was their highest pleasure. That kind does not sit daring the teacher to interest him. That kind does not say, Oh, the hell with it, you can't learn anything from that old hen, she's stupid and boring, and keeps you after school for looking out the window, and picks on some people and makes favorites of others, and blows her nose on her petticoats. Students who complain of boredom are commenting on themselves, not on the class. However bad a teacher is, he knows more than any of his students; and if the second law of thermodynamics has any educational application, there ought to be a flow from the area of higher energy to the area of lower. When there isn't, it isn't always safe to assume that the blockage is at the source. It may be at the destination.

Nevertheless, both schools and teachers may get jittery under criticism and, instead of exposing Johnny to the joys of excellence, set out to turn Johnny on. I am afraid that often the means chosen are the means of the entertainment and advertising industries from which Johnny has got his notions in the first place. We surrender to Johnny's incapacity or laziness by trying to supplement the difficulties of print with audiovisual aids. We let him come at *Moby-Dick* by way of the comic-book version—which is generally as far as he gets. Because he has trouble reading *The Grapes of Wrath*, we organize a visit to the Steinbeck country and have a sort of Steinbeck fiesta at a MacDonalds in Salinas or on Cannery Row. We accept network-TV-watching for credit, we permit book reviews of "Charlie's Angels" or "Hogan's Heroes." We give, and give, and give before his relentless pressure to make work easier. We begin to mug and hoof and court popularity by being cosmetically young and hip, or we grow tight-lipped with resentment at what we are expected to do to our own standards. And whether we give or whether we resist, we displease some students, some parents, some administrators.

So far as I can see, a teacher has no professional obligation to turn his students on. His obligation is to know his subject and teach it. If students want to be entertained, let them go to the beach or the movies. I know: They do, they do! The teacher's obligation is excellence and the pleasures of accomplishment, not entertainment in the usual sense, and students themselves are the first to acknowledge this fact in areas where they don't need motivation. Of a basketball coach they don't demand entertainment—in fact, they will put up with almost unlimited harshness and rigor. His job is to teach skills, and in this case the skills are skills the student wants to learn. How to dribble and shoot and pass, how to set a pick, how to go one on one, how to play zone or man-to-man, how to press and how to

break the press—that is what it's about, and a coach may work
his team's tongues out without drawing complaints. Players respect strictness, because the excellence demanded of them is an
excellence coveted from away back. For this sort of excellence,
moreover, there are rewards both immediate and delayed: the
excitement of competition, the thrill of winning, a limited but
immensely satisfying kind of campus fame. And for a few, a
dazzling future: pro contract, status as a culture hero, fantastic
amounts of money. What a joy it is to a teacher—or would be
—to come upon a student who is motivated in that way toward
the calculus or the use of language! A certain proportion of any
class is so motivated—and makes teaching the profound satisfaction it sometimes is.

I admitted that I don't know anything and have no solutions
to problems. That doesn't prevent me from having prejudices.
My prejudices tell me that the schools have nothing in common with the entertainment industry, and should have nothing
to do with it, and should not try to ingratiate themselves with
students by adopting its methods and standards. My prejudices
tell me that the schools ought to be not the ally of the popular
culture but its principal opponent and alternative. One function of schooling ought to be to develop judgment, perceptiveness, discrimination, the ability to make the fine, subtle,
difficult, encumbered decisions that one is always having to
make in real life. Also the ability to renounce, to give up, to
put gratification second to other, more important matters. Also
the willingness to serve a hard apprenticeship with delayed rewards. The movies and TV teach us to discriminate between
white hats and black hats, but not much else, and their version
of a fine conscience is always canned in heavy syrup. The 3.2
percent psychological perceptions, the 25-watt moral insights,
the interchangeable emotions that are set out for us are the fast
food of the mind—cheeseburgers and fries. They are lousy food,
but even people who know better can develop a taste for them,
and those who don't know any better will accept nothing else.
As by Gresham's Law bad money drives out good, so cheap and
vulgarized and easy fare, either in the fast-food business or in

democratic education, can drive out what is wholesome and nourishing.

How teachers keep the pervasive sex-violence-and-treacle out of the schools is not something my prejudices instruct me about. Or how teachers generate in students the excitement that will make participants of their students, how they overcome the habit of inertia that has come from long hours of sitting in front of the tube like a bucket being filled—there, too, I am no help. Those who have nothing but the popular culture in their background, no concept of the pleasure of intellectual effort, no goals, no curiosity; and especially the rebellious ones, the troublemakers in all their multiple forms—to the teacher who has to deal with them I have nothing to offer but sympathy. They are part of humanity's burden, part of the continuing problem of compulsory universal education, which is the concern of the teaching profession, to which I no longer belong. If I didn't think it can be done I wouldn't even be talking to you; I would have sent flowers. But it is not my immediate problem. My immediate problem concerns the profession to which I do still belong, and which doesn't seem to be doing any better.

This past year, for my sins, I read the best part of the year's supposedly serious novels as a judge for the National Book Awards. It is the only time in my life I have ever read anything like a whole year's production. Like other readers, I usually read the fifteen or twenty that for one reason or other look interesting—because they are written by friends or former students, because a reviewer I respect has given them a good send-off, because they deal with themes or subjects that intrigue me. To read the whole swatch, a couple of hundred of them, is quite another experience, and more daunting. It gives you a sense of the whole field, and the whole field is what daunts me.

Not that they are all bad. On the contrary, individual books are sometimes splendid; talent all up and down the scale. Talent, I've often said, is one of the commonest things that humanity comes up with—much more common than discipline and much more common than skill. We shall have no problem in finding five legitimate and worthy candidates for the Book

Awards when we meet in New York next week, and there are
two dozen books outside of that choice handful that I would
recommend to anyone wanting some nonmedia entertainment
tinged with intelligence. There are others that puzzle me—
which is neither hard to do nor necessarily bad. There are some
that I would not recommend to the most primitive privy,
though they were manifestly written for it.

It bothers me to find that even our best writers, who ought
to be the arbiters of language, people who use the language
best, who say things best—that these novelists, like the schools,
have been affected by the leveling popular culture. Though
they depend upon print, they to some extent demonstrate the
declining authority of print in this oral-pictorial world village
whose arbiters of language, inevitably, have become the TV an-
nouncers and ad writers. Blame TV and Madison Avenue for
some things our novelists do. But also blame the schools—and
include me, for at least twenty of the two hundred books I
have just finished reading were written by my former students,
and they're no more literate than the others.

There have been great novelists without the great gift of
words. Theodore Dreiser never wrote a good sentence in his
life. James Fenimore Cooper set mythic patterns in our fiction
that have lasted to the present, but stylistically remained a
mighty goon. Even Henry James, the darling of some readers,
was described by H. G. Wells as a hippopotamus trying to pick
up a pea. But those men had all the other qualities that make a
novelist—great penetration into character, great understanding
of the human head and the human heart and human scenes—
and one reads them in spite of their defects. I also read many
contemporaries in spite of linguistic inadequacies. If I were
teaching excellence, I would have to urge writers to learn at the
very least correctness and precision. Some of them never do, because the time-spirit of our language is oral, and in an oral culture language changes rapidly, mostly through ignorance or laziness. No matter what the schools may try to do, the tide of
usage is against them; and every now and then a great fortress
such as the Merriam-Webster dictionary surrenders to usage
almost unconditionally. Whatever the most people say is right,

whether it makes sense, whether it blunts discriminations, whatever.

It doesn't much bother me that people who deal daily with data, or work in the media, have never made the discovery that both those words are plural.

It doesn't much bother me that no commentator on the air, apparently, knows that there are two r's in February, and no commentator except Edwin Newman (and Hughes Rudd, who learned it from me) seems to know the difference between lie and lay. It doesn't much trouble me that who and whom are insoluble mysteries to millions. But it does bother my soul when novelists, who along with poets and playwrights ought to be the arbiters of our language, limp along one-eyed, deaf in both ears, mumbling their gums, letting themselves be confused by usage which is simply ignorant.

Lie and lay, for instance: There is only a handful of causative verbs in English: lay, meaning to cause to lie; set, meaning to cause to sit; raise, meaning to cause to rise. They are always transitive—in the active voice they invariably have an object. They are always regular—in terms of the Anglo-Saxon, from which they come, weak—verbs, constructed on the past root of the irregular or strong verb they're related to. They are the one thing I got out of a year studying Anglo-Saxon and a half year of teaching it. I could teach anyone how to deal with them in ten minutes. But such a lord of language as John Updike, to judge by his novel *The Coup*, isn't sure about them, and that bothers my persnickety soul. It's one thing to have egg on some old borrowed tie already stained with a thousand free lunches, but it's another to have it on a white tie above a spotless shirtfront. It makes a good writer look as unwittingly ridiculous as Malvolio coming out cross-gartered and simpering. I feel the same when someone professes to admire my books exceedingly but thinks my name is "Stenger."

Symptoms. Take like and as—already, probably, a lost cause, thanks in part to the deliberate campaign of a Winston ad. Maybe Winston tastes good like a cigarette should, but to say that or say "like I say" indicates that you don't know what the hell language is about. You might as well refer to Shakespeare's

Like You Like It. And if you're that insensitive to prepositions, you don't belong in the writing business. "Between you and I," you'd have a brighter future in Washington. And if you do this sort of thing not out of ignorance but only so as not to seem high-toned or above hoi polloi, then it's worse; then you're like the Englishman who was never unintentionally rude. And the fact that your editor doesn't straighten you out and clean you up only compounds the crime. The whole system of publishing, from writer through editor to critic and general reader, has had its ear for linguistic precision blunted, and I think I know by whom. Or who by, if you prefer.

All that is utterly minor, but symptomatic. Some other things I have run into during my big novel-reading binge interest me much more. If Johnny knew what is in a lot of contemporary novels, Johnny would read. The fact is that print, which used to be somewhat Mrs. Grundyish about strong language and explicit sexual and other acts held to be obscene, has changed at least as fast and as far as the movies, and much farther than TV. How long ago was it—forty years approximately —when Lillian Smith's *Strange Fruit* was banned in Boston, and became the focus of a sensational trial, because of using in two places a certain four-letter word? How long (ten or fifteen years?) since a San Francisco lady poet got in trouble for trying to liberate the "love words." One has the impression now that if the "love words" were removed from some novels it would reduce them to pamphlets. And the obsessive urge toward greater and greater specificity, in sex as in violence, is a pressure that some novelists seem unable to resist. There is a kind of desperation in it, as if novelists felt themselves getting left in the dust. As they are. A very successful novel, a blockbuster, may sell a hundred thousand hard-backed copies. Over the course of years, in paperback, it may sell in the millions. But meantime, how many captive millions is TV reaching? How many million discs does a record by a popular singer or group distribute? What novel is in the class with a movie such as *Superman*, which grosses eighty million dollars in its first month or so?

It is perfectly clear where the money is and where the public acceptance is. True, novels may last longer. A novel such as

The Great Gatsby sold perhaps twenty-five thousand copies in its first edition but has sold millions in reprint since, and has been seen in the movies and on TV and is taught in the schools, an enduring part of the tradition. Still, some novelists are tempted into arenas where they don't belong, into competition with mass media, which have every advantage over them, including fast-food ease of assimilation and a comforting lack of excellence. You might not notice it so plainly if you read only selected novels. Read the whole batch and it is plain that a lot of novelists, including some good ones, have gone into competition not only with the movies and TV but with hard porn. That's confusing. Movies have a code which at least labels their productions; TV has a much stricter code, or the fiction of a code, which pretends to protect child and family viewers. Novels are right out there, undifferentiated. Some of them have *Playboy* dust jackets, many do not. Caveat emptor.

I am not objecting to either the language or the overt sexuality or even the kinky sexuality of these books, in themselves. I would not for a moment go back to the days when novelists wanting to express strong emotion had to write something like d—d, or when, as late as the years of World War II, Hemingway had to go to elaborate wordplay to translate Spanish profanity in *For Whom the Bell Tolls*, and Mailer had to do his four-letter word with a systematic misspelling in *The Naked and the Dead*.

Freedom is a boon, hard won. Every expressive instrument ought to be available to a writer if he is to make the fullest commentary on experience—if he is going to instruct as well as entertain. That does not at all mean that he must use the full extremes of that freedom in every chapter, or even every novel. Some novels, like some lives, may contain no violence, no very heightened scenes. They may be sexually muted, diffident, modest, without being any less true than those which are explicitly erotic.

What the kinky novels lack is a sense of proportion. Reading a batch of them, one gets the impression that all over the United States, in every class and kind and walk of life, men and women are on the prowl for casual sexual partners, and that the less orthodox the partners are, the more representative these sexual *pícaros* and *pícaras* are. But I know hundreds of people, and so do you, who do not fit that pattern at all. I do not see them often in novels. The assumption apparently is that they are not interesting.

Actually the novels of 1978 are overwhelmingly romantic— extreme situations and characters, highly colored events. Even when they pretend to be most offhand, these "sexually inventive" novels are sensational in the worst sense. Their fault is not obscenity but a lack of artistry, for it involves too much of the wrong kind of feeling in the wrong place. I find myself unconvinced by the arguments of a former student, who writes some of the most unbuttoned novels of our time, and who once tried to persuade me that his sexual inventiveness is like the opening of a new continent: "Why, it's a renaissance, man. It's exploring new ground."

The trouble with excessive sexuality, in novels or in life, is that it is so compellingly interesting and attention-holding that it makes everything else seem tame or dull; it crowds off the page whole areas of human experience and human feeling that belong there but can't maintain their foothold. It drives out character—these people aren't characters, they're organs. It drives out human interaction—you have no social relationships, only sexual relationships. It drives out all subtlety of feeling and encourages only the blunt and obtuse. It's artistic suicide to let strong sensations drive out subtle ones. And any fool can do it; that's the worst of it.

Once I had a student, a young lady, who told me her ambition was to write about sex as if it were just like anything else. Yes, I said, but *is* it like everything else? She seemed to think so; I didn't. In more than one way, sex is climactic; and if you have a bout of fellatio on page three, it's a little hard to follow the act with anything that will top it. Moreover, if you tip your hand early, you are going to drive away whole audiences, including some of the best and most intelligent. They will think you are misrepresenting American life, because their own lives do not contain such capers and they refuse to think that in spite of manuals like *The Sensuous Woman* very many American lives do contain them.

The other day, I was talking to a bookseller in Palo Alto, an elderly lady who has loved books all her life and sold hundreds of thousands of them to all sorts of customers. I had just come from a debauch with a lot of kinky novels, and I asked her what on earth I ought to do with them when this competition is over. Ordinarily, I give a lot of books every year to the public libraries in our area, but some of those I had been reading seemed to me not quite what the public libraries would want. "I throw a lot of my examination copies in the wastebasket," she said—a horrible thing for a booklover to say—"and the ones that are within reason I give to the Veterans hospital, on the theory that those folks are hardened."

So I made up my mind that I would take my two hundred novels, or all but a couple of dozen of them, to the VA hospital. Throwing them in the wastebasket would hurt my sensibilities as much as burning them would do. But the next afternoon, I was at a tea at one of the public libraries, and I mentioned to the librarian what I was going to do, and why. She all but cried. "Oh, dear," she said. "All of them? You'd be surprised what some of our customers want."

So I will let her take her pick before I head for the hospital. Maybe she will want them all. If she does, I will know that the revolution has passed me completely by, that the principles of restraint, proportion, and a wide representation of all kinds of life—the literary principles I have tried to live and write by— have all been overtaken and overwhelmed, and that the great snollygoster of the mass media, which has a propeller in its tail, has whipped us all into a homogenized batter. I have tried, on occasion, to get as much mileage out of a kiss as some novelists get out of an orgy, and I will have to go on doing it that way or stop writing. Maybe my ex-student is right about the renaissance country of sexuality, and the exhilaration of having no limits. On the other hand, I am stubborn enough to wait with some confidence for the exploiters to make even sex tedious, and for the American public with some wider notion of excellence—writers and readers, teachers and booksellers, editors and critics—to react toward sanity. The curious thing about America is that it generally does recover from its excesses. We threaten to breed ourselves clear out of the agar dish, and just when the demographers are predicting that by 2020 there will be only two square yards of earth for each of us, we get the message and the birthrate drops through the floor. Just when we're all in danger of dying of heart attacks, we get the message and start eating sensibly and jogging. Just when Lake Erie seems permanently dead with sludge and pollution, we wake up and start bringing it back to health. And just when the sexologists are on the brink of cheapening and demoralizing an urge that should be private and close to holy, maybe we will turn that around too. Maybe the schools can turn it around and provide models of conduct more permanently sound than rock stars, TV personalities, instant celebrities, sexual *pícaros*, and the rest. Once, I remember, Ralph Waldo Emerson and self-reliance were an inspiration to whole generations of Americans, including some who were a long way from being readers and thinkers. Whom do we have now? Hugh Hefner? I don't think he can last.

The Pleasure Principle, according to Freud, leads us to try to achieve satisfaction of our desires through fantasy. That is the whole secret behind the phenomenal success of *Playboy*. That mystery explains the movies. It explains the giveaway shows in which Fortune drops two weeks in Hawaii on you for naming correctly the names of the four Beatles. The opposite of the Pleasure Principle, Freud said, is the Reality Principle, which leads us to look at things as they are, to cut back our expectations, to ask for less.

Good-bye to All T--t!

Not everyone who laments what contemporary novelists have done to the sex act objects to the act itself, or to its mention. Some want it valued higher than fiction seems to value it; they want the word "climax" to retain some of its literary meaning. Likewise, not everyone who has come to doubt the contemporary freedom of language objects to strong language in itself. Some of us object precisely because we value it.

I acknowledge that I have used four-letter words familiarly all my life, and have put them into books with some sense that I was insisting on the proper freedom of the artist. I have applauded the extinction of those d---d emasculations of the genteel tradition and the intrusion into serious fiction of honest words with honest meanings and emphasis. I have wished, with D. H. Lawrence, for the courage to say shit before a lady, and have sometimes had my wish.

Words are not obscene: Naming things is a legitimate verbal act. And "frank" does not mean "vulgar," any more than "improper" means "dirty." What vulgar does mean is "common"; what improper means is "unsuitable." Under the right circumstances, any word is proper. But when any sort of word, especially a word hitherto taboo and therefore noticeable, is scattered across a page like chocolate chips through a Toll House cookie, a real impropriety occurs. The sin is not the use of an "obscene" word; it is the use of a loaded word in the wrong place or in the wrong quantity. It is the sin of false emphasis, which is not a moral but a literary lapse related to sentimentality. It is the sin of advertisers who so plaster a highway with neon signs that you can't find the bar or liquor store you're looking for. Like any excess, it quickly becomes comic.

If I habitually say shit before a lady, what do I say before a flat tire at the rush hour in Times Square or on the San Francisco Bay Bridge? What do I say before a revelation of the inequity of the universe? And what if the lady takes the bit in her teeth and says shit before *me?*

I have been a teacher of writing for many years and have watched this problem since it was no bigger than a man's hand. It used to be that, with some Howellsian notion of the young-girl audience, one tried to protect tender female members of a mixed class from the coarse language of males trying to show off. Some years ago Frank O'Connor and I agreed on a system. Since we had no intention whatever of restricting students' choice of subject or language, and no desire to expurgate or bowdlerize while reading their stuff aloud for discussion, but at the same time had to deal with these young girls of an age our daughters might have been, we announced that any stuff so strong that it would embarrass us to read it aloud could be read by its own author.

It was no deterrent at all, but an invitation, and not only to coarse males. For clinical sexual observation, for full acceptance of the natural functions, for discrimination in the selection of graffiti, for boldness in the use of words that it should take courage to say before a lady, give me a sophomore girl every time. Her strength is as the strength of ten, for she assumes that if one shocker out of her pretty mouth is piquant, fifty will be literature. And so do a lot of her literary idols.

Some acts, like some words, were never meant to be casual. That is why houses contain bedrooms and bathrooms. Profanity and so-called obscenities are literary resources, verbal ways of rendering strong emotion. They are not meant to occur every ten seconds, any more than—Norman Mailer to the contrary notwithstanding—orgasms are.

So I am not going to say shit before any more ladies. I am

going to hunt words that have not lost their sting, and it may be I shall have to go back to gentility to find them. Pleasant though it is to know that finally a writer can make use of any word that fits his occasion, I am going to investigate the possibilities latent in restraint.

I remember my uncle, a farmer who had used four-letter words ten to the sentence ever since he learned to talk. One day he came too near the circular saw and cut half his fingers off. While we stared in horror, he stood watching the bright arterial blood pump from his ruined hand. Then he spoke, and he did not speak loud. "Aw, the dickens," he said.

I think he understood, better than some sophomore girls and better than some novelists, the nature of emphasis.

PART II

That New Man,
the American

If we lived in another sort of society—if the university were a *kiva*, say, and professors were Hopi elders, and students were young people being initiated into the rituals, obligations, roles, and duties of their adult lives, the instruction of the young would be blissfully simple. Professors would be teaching what their teachers had taught them, and would know it for truth and never doubt it. Students would accept it gratefully and humbly and with a sense of entering into the full meaning and satisfaction of their lives. If this were a simple, traditional society, we would all be looking backward, not forward, and we would be agreed on what we believe.

This is not to ignore the groups all over America, the churches especially, that maintain their own coherent system of belief and conduct within the surrounding complexity. But every such system is exposed to challenge from other systems. Historically, our groups and sects have tended to be swamped or diluted from without, or else to grow rigid in self-defense. And the great majority of Americans no longer belong to any such traditional group. We all live in a complex, pluralistic society which began in revolution against authority and in adaptation to an unknown continent; which throughout its history has had poured into it unassimilated and perhaps unassimilable ethnic and cultural elements; and which has consistently challenged its own traditions as fast as it has made them.

Despite a certain sentimental cherishing of our past, we do not consult it much except to justify innovation. Our past is as hard to make into a single thing as our present is. American industry added to the industrial revolution not only the principle of mass production with interchangeable parts but the counterprinciple of annual retooling. American society at large exhibits the same contradiction. On the one hand, it has been sedulous to produce a national type, or stereotype—the "new man" we have been trying to define ever since Crèvecoeur. On the other, it has applied to conventions and popular culture Jefferson's suggestion—which he meant politically—of a revolution every generation. What gives some of us future shock is only a speedup; our revolutions now happen every five years.

From the beginning of this republic, we have heard that democratic society works toward standardization, a sameness of character and response, a leveling toward mediocrity and stereotype. That was a piece of European snobbery that we let ourselves be taken in by. Nothing could be wronger. By comparison with almost any nation that could be named, we are the wildest mixture, or nonmixture, of races, creeds, colors, economic systems, political systems, behavioral patterns, regional types, and cultures. Though we are swept by fads, every fad breeds its counterfad. Our life-styles are so ferociously various that our reaction to a style not our own—and we may find it next door or in our own family—may be anything from apathy to disgust. It is not simply a polarization between old and young, though that is part of it and always has been. There are not two sides to every question, but a dozen or a hundred. American life is not a conflict between conservative and liberal, black and white, establishment and counterculture, work ethic and pleasure principle. It is a blindfold battle royal. You may hit anybody you run into.

The tendency to experimentation, rebellion, and nonconformity grows stronger, not weaker. The civil rights struggle and Vietnam only intensified what would have been there without them. There is so much articulate dissatisfaction, so much variety and freedom in dress, speech, literature, sexual and family relations, education, politics, and attitudes toward all authority, that it strikes the conservative as anarchy and would appall a Hopi elder. Those who exercise those freedoms call those who are appalled the Establishment; those called the Establishment are often too appalled to find a name for what appalls them, though they think plenty. And both Establishment and Counterestablishment are many things, not one. The Establishment is everything from the Pentagon to the grading system of a university. The Counterestablishment is everything from a church vigil against war to political assassination.

If you have a taste for history, as most Americans do not, you can look back and find a Protestant, middle-class core devoted to the work ethic, which in various places has managed for a time to become a sort of American orthodoxy. But it has varied from class to class, region to region. It was never so dominant as it wanted to be, and it was constantly challenged by reformist, non-Christian, radical, or simply crackpot ideas, variations on a theme of dissent. A lot of things the radicals of the 1970s thought they had invented were as historical and American as the profit motive or the Congregational Church.

As surely as the latest hippy cluster, Plymouth Colony was a commune. So was Far West, Missouri; so was Nauvoo, Illinois. So were New Harmony, Fruitlands, Brook Farm, the Oneida Community, and the Shaker town at Watervliet, New York. So were the Fourierist and Owenite communities; so were the Dukhobor and Mennonite and Dunkard groups scattered across the United States and Canada. The yearning to bring about the perfected society of men has been a constant since the seventeenth century. But perfection has had many experimental varieties that have warred with one another and sometimes with sweet reason.

And they repeat one another. People isolated on frontiers without the comforts and consolations of a settled society felt a great need both for the company of others and for peace in their own spirits. Religious revivals served both needs, often at a high temperature. People got the jerks, spoke in tongues, underwent passionate conversions, and undoubtedly benefited psychologically, whatever the wear and tear. The same people now, lost in the anonymity of cities, find a sort of communion through Esalen or EST or encounter groups. Or they drop out of a complex society into a simpler one, join Venceremos or become street people or neo-Nazis, and within the real coerciveness of those antisystems purge their emotions by building people's parks or throwing rocks at cops. Or they get a big purge at rock festivals, or sit cross-legged in Zen meditation, sometimes on TV.

Or consider bread. Generations ago, some Americans got a mystic comfort out of Graham's bread, which was filled with bran and shorts and other healthful horse food, and which went counter to the trend toward purified conformity. Their crusade lost out to commercial bakeries that went on to produce the world's worst and most expensive and least nourishing loaf. But for some years health bread has been back, with all its bran and mysticism and with a lot more—pine nuts and oat hulls and acorns—all stone-ground and certified by Adelle Davis.

Almost as much as in the 1830s, Jesus freaks are a fact of life. Universities, Stanford included, have heard undergraduates talking in tongues. Student activists recently took to the streets with the same angers that fired their great-grandfathers during the draft riots of the Civil War. The antagonisms between them and their parents are the same arguments, only intensified, that raged between us and our parents in the 1920s. The drug scene reproduces many of the anguishes, confrontations, and experiments that Prohibition produced. As a comfort to contemporary parents, let me confess that in Salt Lake City in the 1920s I knew boys who drank a mixture of gasoline and milk because they had heard it was intoxicating, and others who habitually put ether in home brew because they *knew* it was intoxicating. Some survived to become parents.

Before the New Left was born, I knew Young Communist League people, and I have studied the IWW, and I can testify that the Wobblies and the YCL differed by hardly a comma in vehemence, True Believer temperament, and conviction of virtue, from the young people who day before yesterday were trashing windows and burning cars at Stanford and Berkeley. Even the tactics repeat the direct action, sabotage, and flooding of the jails that the IWW found effective, and the outright terrorists are blood brothers to the Molly Maguires.

Even rebellion, that is, can be standardized, cyclic, repetitive, and mass-produced with interchangeable parts, but that is not the truth I want to emphasize. My point is that many options are open, and have always been open—political, religious, moral, social, and institutional. The tyranny of the majority has always been challengeable within the rules, and has been persistently challenged, often violently, often foolishly and unwisely. It has been both our strength and our weakness that custom and conservatism have never for long been able to shut off dissent and experimentation.

What faces young Americans today is not ritual submission to the truths of the elders, nor is it repudiation of the elders' truth. It is the same old drastic, difficult, uncertain, historically American problem of multiple choice without a norm against which choice may be checked, of liberty that permits even the enemies of liberty a lot of rope. Our very tradition teaches us to question everything, or nearly everything.

The unexamined life, according to Plato's *Apology*, is not worth living. We may go further. The unexamined society is an ant society. Tradition, like the majority, may become a tyrant. But to question does not mean to repudiate—not necessarily. Unlikely as it sometimes seems, there may be things in our social and political structure worth hanging onto. Rituals, codes, folkways, roles, legends, conformities are a limitation of tribal societies, but at the same time, for the individuals living in such societies, they are the most profoundly comforting source of security. The necessity to question and challenge has been the greatest strength of the American system, but it has helped make this remarkably successful country poor in personal satisfactions, productive too often of fear, loneliness, and *anomie*.

Any human society is held together mainly by nonrational bonds—by sentiments, folkways, habits established by accident and preserved by inertia. No man has ever lived in the perfected society. Any of us could make a social blueprint that would improve upon what we have. The trouble is, it wouldn't work, not even in experimental America. The bloodiest revolutions change little—the wave passes on and the water remains; the king is thrown out of the colonies and the habits that stem from Magna Carta and the Witenagemot remain.

Logical and empirical thinking may profoundly affect human institutions, as the Bill of Rights (itself a codification of habits and assumptions) has affected America. But once established, those principles are not experimental; they are taken for granted. A man may think experimentally within narrow limits, say the limits of his science or profession, but outside he is likely to be guided by uniformities of action into which he never inquires. Moreover, most experiments, like most mutations, are monsters, and cannot live. As Pareto says, even within a limited field people have trouble thinking experimentally unless they are supported on all sides by a wider, nonlogical discipline that need not be questioned. While we are challenging our party structure or our marriage customs, we take the Bill of Rights for granted. Even the American Maoists erected their revolution on that platform. And a good thing, too, that at least this much is stable. If we retooled our Constitution as often as we retool our factories and our social and sexual conventions, we would be *really* anxious.

The melting pot has not fully worked, the standardized mediocrity that even acute European observers predicted for us has proved a bugbear. If we perish, we will perish of diversity, choice, and change, rather than of standardization. Standardization we could use a little more of. As Whitehead remarked, "Unless society is permeated, through and through, with routine, civilization vanishes."

Routine. It is an odd thing to recommend to a people hooked on novelty, inured to experiment and rebellion. It sounds dull. It smacks of the work ethic, not the pleasure principle. But plenty of Americans feel, and have always felt, the attractiveness of systems that do not call for constant choice. Some use their liberties to create systems that restrict liberty, and so try to regain the certainty that multiple choice has cost them.

It is that urge that drives people to drop out and live by their hands beyond the Arctic Circle. Peace Corps volunteers are moved by it, though they may carry with them the infection from which they flee. New Left, rigid Right, the war hawks—all evade the bewilderment of liberty by accepting the simplicities of a revolutionary, fascist, or martial order. Hippies and drug-culture people feel it, whether they reach for the ultimate simplicity of acid or camp out in a wash below Taos Pueblo and beg the Indians to teach them how to worship the earth in dance. I suppose all mortals yearn for a peaceful simplicity at times. Americans have more cause to than most. A lot of our experimentation toward the perfected society is an attempt to escape the complexities of our freedom to experiment.

And yet something else is at work in us too. Watch us abroad. We tend to bad-mouth ourselves; we feel our lack of cathedrals; we look upon European cultures, all of them far more traditional than ours, as somehow superior. We rush abroad by millions, swearing we want to avoid the American tourist. But let us meet a fellow American in Trafalgar Square or La Ciotat or in the bazaar of Shiraz and we may respond with unexpected friendliness. We compare notes, we swap experiences and adventures and addresses. We haunt the kiosks for the latest Paris *Herald Tribune* to see how the Giants did. There is more recognizable American-ness in us than we often acknowledge, and in a strange land, among strangers, we respond automatically, not experimentally, to what we recognize and know. That compulsion worked even upon voluntary exiles from the draft in Canada and Sweden. Despite their hatred of what drove them away, most wanted to come home, they valued something in the system that bred them. Else what was the amnesty problem about?

So if I were that Hopi-elder professor and some student came asking my advice about how to live in his native land, what would I tell him? Only a few things, and even those made difficult by the necessity of choice.

1) Question the act of questioning. To question does not

necessarily mean to repudiate. Think things over, but think a long time before you kick them over, for your liberties may be inside. When students disrupted the classes of William Shockley at Stanford because of his racial theories, which are repugnant to me and to everyone I know and which are understandably infuriating to black and Third World students, they kicked over the bucket that holds their own freedom. If they can shut Shockley up, somebody can shut *them* up. Freedom of speech implies the freedom of unpopular, even grotesque and repulsive speech, or it is no freedom at all.

2) Question the questioner. We are all likely to blame the system, the military-industrial complex, the multiversity, or something else for what is weak or wrong in ourselves. The aim of our lives, so far as I can see, is conduct, not behavior; and conduct is not a galvanic twitch in response to stimuli, but activity guided by a code of personal ethics and an obligation of personal integrity. There are some things too dishonest or self-indulgent or socially harmful for a good man to do. It is a lesson that might have been posted on the walls of some Nixon White House offices. Knowing what is shameful and unworthy is more important than affiliation with any cause or the experience of any pleasure. But knowing it and acting on it involves the hardest choices of anyone's life.

3) Question perfection. Idealism is almost invariably self-righteous. The late Bernard DeVoto called it "a cross-lots path to Berchtesgaden and St. Bartholomew's Eve." Militant idealism tends to end with a machine gun in its hands, or else, balked from coercing others into right thinking, it withdraws in disgust and tries to create one of those enclaves of perfection where the handouts grow on bushes and the little streams of alcohol come trickling down the rocks. Those enclaves are too ideal to be lived in by the damned human race, and it is dangerous to dream them at more than about 3.2 percent.

We are citizens of the freest (and hence most dangerous), most complicated, fastest-changing, and most experimental society the world has ever seen. We complicate it further by refusing to pay any attention to our history and so are constantly repeating the experiments of the past, including the failed ones.

The millennium has come and gone a hundred times in our history. We should kiss it good-bye. What we should expect is more of what we have had: the clashing, shifting, violent, dynamic equilibrium of a thousand variable forces, tendencies, peoples, religions, aspirations, and at our core a small, indisputable, perhaps slowly growing nucleus of law that guarantees our anarchy and our idealism as well as our soberer efforts toward a workable and possibly just society.

We are built like an atom, as a matter of fact, and we bombard ourselves with a steady electron stream of questioning and dissent. An elder can suggest what the nucleus contains, and admit reluctantly that even the nucleus is open to bombardment. Go ahead, see what particles can be knocked off. But understand that the nucleus is bombarded at the bombardier's own risk. For somewhere in there, in that basic Bill of Rights and in the minimal unanimity we have achieved as "that new man, the American," is our unity as a people and culture, and our hope as a nation. It is not to be attacked lightly, for fear some random electron might knock off the quark without which nothing would run or hold together. And yet the nucleus is not by itself the whole hope either. What holds us together is the electrical charge, the tension between the positive core of our tradition and the negatively charged electrons of challenge and choice and change.

The Provincial
Consciousness

The last thing I would try to do is to instruct Canadians in their own culture, rebuke them for not having one, or tell them how to handle either their internal cultural problems or their relations with the powerful neighbor who provides them about equally with things they don't want and things they can't do without, examples they deplore and temptations they can't resist.

All I will try to do is tell you how the present state of Canadian culture appears to a visitor of barely two months, and to suggest some American parallels, both historic and contemporary. They may provide either horrible examples or the sort of comfort and encouragement harried parents feel when they read Spock or Gesell and find that almost *all* fifteen-year-olds act that way. At worst, it may infuriate some Canadians by suggesting that even in the matter of cultural inferiority complexes the United States has to insist that it got there first, and that Canada, as usual, is compulsively repeating American experience two generations or more behind.

I don't want to infuriate anyone, and though I will defend the United States on most counts, I don't come as a Yankee freebooter bent upon annexing Canada. If there was ever a manifest destinarian in me, he exhausted himself on the way West and doesn't operate north-south. Moreover, my loyalties are mixed, for I spent a half dozen of my most impressionable years on a Saskatchewan homestead and missed becoming a Canadian by only about one inch of rain. So if I say something detestable, please remember that I am trying to speak simultaneously from within and without the family. I am an American visitor, but also I am a kind of knot-headed country cousin, more to be pitied than censured, and more to be loved than reviled.

Let me summarize how the Canadian literary scene strikes the visitor. None of this will be new to you, but you ought to know the conceptions from which I begin.

First, there is an extraordinary stir, great activity, great interest, and a frequent and often assertive use of the word "Canadian." One finds all kinds of little magazines, many of them with a nationalist or ethnic cast, and even the larger-circulation magazines like *Maclean's*, even the newspapers, reflect patriotic cultural ideas. The legislature wants Ontario's colleges to get their faculties up to at least 80 percent Canadian, there is a drive to get more Canadian books taught in the schools. The bulletin boards announce poetry readings, lectures, symposia, debates, seminars. I had hardly arrived on the University of Toronto campus and been handed my free New Testament before someone topped it with a book entitled *Read Canadian*. The bookstores and libraries feature whole sections of Canadian books, the book-review pages are alert to cover new ones. There seems to be an extensive series of grants, prizes, and awards to encourage Canadian writers and Canadian publishers, and one whole paperback library lines up all the Canadians together like garden gods. It is exhilarating to be in a place where literature is taken seriously by so many kinds of people.

Second, one is struck by the identity crisis Canada seems to be going through—seems to have been going through ever since World War II, when the bond with Britain finally wore thin. I have talked to those who are determined to discover a Cana-

dian identity (and assume it or invent it if necessary) and those
who doubt there is any such thing. National characteristics, always elusive, have been rounded up like cattle on the range,
and are kept milling in a cloud of dust, but there are skeptics
who insist that they're rustled stock, that none of them wears a
clear Canadian brand; they all have burns or earmarks that declare them English, or American, or ethnic.

Nobody seems to think any more that a Canadian is a colo-
nial Englishman, and almost everybody seems determined that
he shall not be a provincial American, but any positive attempt
to define him runs head on into the abiding division between
the French and the British Canadas, so that if there is an identity it is a divided one. I don't suppose it helps the state of
mind of English-speaking Canada to be aware that of the two
Canadas the French has the clearer character. It has a language, called debased but still its own, that marks it off from
both English Canada and France; and it has a culture that has
been developing in relative isolation ever since Louis XV abandoned Québec to its fate. Culturally, that isolation may have
been good for it, and it could be on the brink of brilliant pro-
ductiveness.

But defining English Canada is like wrapping four water-
melons. The differences, even the antipathies, between Ontario
and British Columbia, the Prairie Provinces, and the Maritimes
may not be as acute as those between Ontario and Québec,
but they are real; and the mosaic theory, Canada's answer to
the melting pot, actively promotes not unity but diversity of
culture. As Northrop Frye has pointed out, those who assert a
unitary identity risk being absurd, while those who assume that
true identity is either regional or ethnic are on their way to
balkanization and—he seems to fear—separatism.

There are those who believe that the physical environment
and climate exert an irresistible torque upon people over a period of time, shaping both their way of life and their character.
I tend to think so myself. Yet the other night I had a stirring
argument with an economist from Saskatchewan, where I
would have thought the environmental determinism most de-
monstrable, who insisted that culture creates geography, not

the other way around. Furthermore, there is a large contingent of Canadians, resigned or bitter, who feel that American mass culture has already so infiltrated Canadian society that it can never be Canadian, but will always be some variant of the global village culture described by Marshall McLuhan. It is said that Canada comes too late in communications history to develop an indigenous culture.

When discussing the identity drive, one should not forget those who espouse the rather desperate faith that the Canadian character has been shaped throughout its history by contact with the wilderness. The first book I read when I began to read Canadian was an anthology of Canadian writing called *Marked by the Wild*. It contained many things that I was glad to read, but I don't think it proved its thesis, which seemed to be that the wilderness has set its seal upon Canadian hearts, and that if one looks and listens and reads carefully, one will discover that all Canadians are mystically one and that the sound of canoe paddles echoes through books as various as those by Morley Callaghan, W. O. Mitchell, and Marie-Claire Blais. I exaggerate, of course; but even if the thesis could be demonstrated, it is hard to see how the Canadian identity could be differentiated by that test from the American; for Americans, too, especially in the West, still try to define their character as an inheritance from the frontier.

I seem to find in Toronto a good deal not only of literary patriotism but also of what a nationalist would probably call cultural defeatism: the belief that, never having had a revolution, nor even a frontier in the stripped-down American sense, English Canada (or at least Ontario) has been a garrison society, dedicated to remaining British in a far land, and conservative and anachronistic British at that; and that when it did begin to grow away from England it was already in the stranglehold of the United States. I hear that, perhaps as a consequence, English Canada has produced no heroes or archetypal figures. I hear that it has no language of its own, only residual British, now fading, and borrowed American; and that even its one claim to specialness, its pronunciation of the sound "out," may be heard in the Virginia tidewater. I hear that Canadian literature, despite its patriotic fervors, does not compete in the big leagues. I hear Mordecai Richler, one of its better novelists, joking sourly about being "world famous all over Canada." I read one of Canada's distinguished critics to the effect that "if evaluation were one's guiding principle . . . criticism of Canadian literature would become only a debunking project."

Along with the patriotism and the defeatism, the overpraise and underpraise of Canadian writing, the American visitor can't miss the widespread, sometimes savage hostility to the United States. It surprises him, not that he wants to defend Watergate, Vietnam, economic and cultural bullying, and exploitation of another nation's resources, or applaud the perpetuation in Canada of a branch-plant economy, or approve the domination of Canadian publishing by American firms which add insult to injury by overcharging Canadians for their imported books. And not because he likes American TV programs any better than his Canadian brother, or the advertising that in Bill Mitchell's words seems so often to present professional models confiding more than one cares to know about their armpits. He is only dismayed to find himself attacked for things he dislikes just as much as Canadians do. And he keeps running into ambivalent responses like the letter to the editor I saw some weeks ago asking angrily why the detestable programs from below the border are always so much more professional and entertaining than Canadian attempts to compete with them. That attitude reminds me irresistibly of the distinguished Massachusetts Republican with whom I listened to radio returns of the 1940 presidential election. When it was clear that Roosevelt had won again, he poured himself a drink and said, "The son of a bitch may be our greatest President."

Gnashings of teeth, beatings of breasts, skepticism and aspiration, ambition and impotence, cultural dependence bitter toward what enslaves it or protesting too much its independence, a double preoccupation with who one is and what others think of one, an abiding desire to make it in the American world and a reiterated indifference to that world, these are the stigmata of the provincial state of mind. Toronto is an authentic capital, a world city, and Ontario is a province which within the Canadian sphere is more potent than any half dozen states within the American. But many of its artists and intellectuals obviously feel that it is an outlier of the English-speaking world, culturally a province, and it responds to its anxieties in the way provinces always have and always will. Provincialism and nationalist fervor are aspects or stages of the same thing.

At the end of its first war with Great Britain, and even more frenetically after its second, the United States was busy hunting down its native identity and asserting its cultural independence. It reacted furiously to English snobbery and condescension, it went around like the Chinese farmer pulling up its rice plants to see how they were growing. Pick up Robert Spiller's anthology *The American Literary Revolution, 1783–1837*, and read in Royall Tyler, Joel Barlow, Timothy Dwight, Noah Webster, and the group who created *The North American Review* sentiments very like those I heard in a conference on Problems in Canadian Literature. Read Crèvecoeur's *Letters from an American Farmer*, with its reverberating question "Who is the American, this new man?" and with the change of a name you might think yourself in contemporary Canada. "Who is this other new man, the Canadian, and how has he evolved away from the earlier new man?" Read Tocqueville's *Democracy in America*, and among much sympathetic observation of American institutions and customs you will find expressed the fear of democratic leveling, the fear of cultural and intellectual mediocrity, the fear of a "homogenized" society, to take a word from Canadian critics, that makes many Canadians uneasy about following in American tracks.

The North American Review believed that the future belonged to America, the brash young giant of the New World; I hear Canadians saying that the twenty-first century belongs to Canada. All through the nineteenth century, the notion of American innocence as contrasted with European corruption was an abiding theme in American writing and a constant in Americans' notion of themselves (it crops up again in regional terms as late as *The Great Gatsby*). It crops up also in Canada. Canadians, it is said, have never been guilty of the violence, disorder, and corruption prevalent below the line; Canadians are simply more *moral* than Americans, a more decent and less rapacious breed.

The debates about language that agitated the United States in the late-eighteenth century have been spared English Canada, and in a way that is Canada's loss. They don't have a language to rally around, they don't need a Noah Webster to legitimize their speech. They have been speaking North American for a long time, and I hear few Anglophile or purist Canadians rebuking their countrymen in the way James Fenimore Cooper rebuked his: for such barbarities as saying "cucumber" instead of the mellifluous and correct "cowcumber." But I hear all that going on in Québec, in the disputes between the *joual* group, who accept a humiliating and debased language and resolve to lift it into legitimacy and eloquence, and those who cling to "good" French. On the strength of historical precedent I would put my money on *joual*, and bet that before too long some Chaucer, Rabelais, Mark Twain, or Bjørnstjerne Bjørnson will come along to show *joual* capable of every effect a writer can ask of it, a vernacular matured from below into a "national" language.

Writers of the early nationalistic period in the United States had cause to lament their cultural poverty. They tried to transplant elegances and they tried to transfer forms developed in the old country to American subject matters. Hence the epics about Niagara Falls and Daniel Boone, hence the blank verse, the Addisonian prose, the togas on the statues of statesmen. Nevertheless the cultural cupboard was pretty bare, and both Hawthorne and James, in successive generations, lamented it. Hawthorne tried what seems to me the better alternative when he made an effort to create a usable past; James took the route of expatriation. Not all of this is apposite to modern Canada. Canadians don't feel *culturally* inferior to the United States, as Americans felt culturally inferior to England. Some look down on the corrupt, vulgar, plastic culture to the south with as much disdain as British travelers in the 1840s did. It could be that their attitude is residual-British, rather than Canadian, a survival of the garrison mind, and it could be that it is more prevalent in Ontario than in western Canada, and it could be that it is guilty of looking on the United States as a monolith. No matter. It is somewhat different from the provincial inferiority feeling of the young American republic. And yet Hugh MacLennan spent half the space of his first novel, *Barometer Rising*, establishing Halifax as a legitimate setting for fiction, and I think I detect some of the same impulse, less obtrusively handled, in the novels of Robertson Davies about Ontario cities. And many Canadians have elected expatriation, either to Europe or to the United States. Perhaps the brain drain shows signs of reversing itself, as the drain from the United States to England has reversed itself in the past quarter century, but it still seems at worst or best a two-way flow, about a standoff.

In 1837, Emerson delivered in Cambridge his celebrated address "The American Scholar," with its declaration of cultural independence: "We have listened too long to the courtly muses of Europe." That was fifty years after the first wasp-nest stirrings of American cultural nationalism, and Emerson's declaration did not mean that the battle was won, by any means. Irving had transplanted some German legends to the Hudson Valley, and Cooper (the American Scott, we called him proudly) had for lack of any American society turned to the sea and the forest, and within the American wilderness had created one of the great archetypal figures of American identity, Leatherstocking. And Hawthorne and Poe had begun to fashion the form of the modern short story. But by comparison with England, American literature in 1837 could show only what one critic called "a few, dim, blinking lights." Cultural identity, the cultural independence of a new country, is not won in a day, or in fifty years. It could be provocatively asserted, and plausibly defended, that Canada in 1974 is somewhere around the stage of self-definition and literary accomplishment reached by the U.S.A. about 1837.

But again, if Canadians are anxious, there is instruction in history. America in 1837 had little to be confidently proud of in its literature, and only foreshadowings of a national identity. Wait twenty-five years and there are *The Scarlet Letter*, *Leaves of Grass*, *Moby-Dick*, the books of the great romantic historians. Wait another twenty-five and there are *Huckleberry Finn*, much of James and Howells, a whole broad pyramid base of secondary writers. There is applause from abroad, the sweetest music that cultural nationalism knows. And there is a whole gallery of figures who in one way or other might represent Crèvecoeur's "new man," the American. They run all the way from Uncle Sam and the Yankee types who begin with Royall Tyler's play *The Contrast*, through Leatherstocking and all the Boone-Crockett-Carson-Bridger avatars of Leatherstocking, and on to Lincoln, Mark Twain, Howells, and still on to the literary creation Henry James called Christopher Newman, in *The American*.

I would like to emphasize that it did take a hundred years and the efforts of four generations of writers, some of them writers of the highest genius, to answer Crèvecoeur's question. And by the time the ink was dry on *The American*, the trial synthesis represented by Newman—a Wasp with democratic, frontier, and business overlays and with a plentiful supply of American naïveté, American innocence, and American integrity —was already obsolete. There would have to be new and larger syntheses, taking account of vast non-Wasp immigrations, the closing of the frontier, the rapid industrialization and urbanization of the country, the emergence of new regions, and a considerable loss of innocence. And following that, still another synthesis allowing for the recalcitrant elements that the melting pot never melted down, the stubborn and persistent subcultures of Blacks, Chicanos, Indians, Orientals, to some extent the Boston Irish, to some extent the Jews.

Those syntheses have not yet come about, and I doubt that they will, short of the millennium. The nation is made up of too many kinds. The archetypal figures of the American have been limited by region, by ethnic background, by chronology, or by all three. And just about when people gave up trying to synthesize an archetypal American, they gave up calling for the Great American Novel. It began to be clear that our Yankees, Leatherstockings, pikes, rednecks, Hoosiers, our Webfeet and Mormons and Hispanos and cowboys and steamboatmen and railroaders derived from a region or an occupation or a stage of the frontier, not from the nation as a whole. Folklore and local color exploited them all, both romantically and realistically, and it emphasized not the American-ness that made them vaguely alike but the picturesque differences that divided them.

Local color was the literary fashion from the early 1860s to the turn of the century. Its romantic and picturesque elements then went somewhat out of fashion, but American literature in the twentieth century has been dominated by a series of sectionalisms either geographical or ethnic: the Midwesterners in the twenties, the Southerners on their heels, the New York school on the heels of the Southerners, the Blacks on the heels of the New Yorkers. Regional or ethnic, they have had things in common. Check the writings of the *Fugitive* group that wrote the script for the South, especially such a book as the symposium *I'll Take My Stand* or Donald Davidson's unreconstructed blast at New York *The Attack on Leviathan*, and you see writers making a hate object out of New York, as the early American nationalists made one out of England and Canadians tend to make one out of the United States, monolithically conceived, and the Quebeckers make one out of English Canada. The Midwest was similarly suspicious of New York, and still is; so are the Far West and the other regions. As for black writers, they fill the space marked "Hate Me" with a vague malevolent face of Whitey and tend to rally around a language, Black English, in a society of soul brothers.

Every successive group, pulling itself out of the regional mud or out of the anonymity of the ghettos, has defined itself in opposition to something. Every such group that I know anything about has been guilty of back scratching, praising its own crowd, forming a countercoterie against the reigning one. There is a lot of that today among writers in the West, who feel, not without provocation, that the reigning New York clique ignores both them and their region. Because I am a Westerner and was once a sort of Midwesterner, I have shared those resentments. The other night, when a somewhat heated Canadian nationalist told me he'd rather live in Saudi Arabia, which he described as a benevolent dictatorship, than in the United States, I had to disagree with him; but if he'd said New

York I might have agreed. I take some pleasure in the statistics showing that only 13 percent of Americans living in the largest American cities *want* to live there. Zoos, full of hostile, over-sexed, and dangerous zoo animals; the dismal sewers into which the American dream has finally run. But there are other Americas than the great cities, newer and better ones than New York, which is hardly an American city at all. The twenty-first century may belong to Canada, but it will have to share it with the western United States, which is about as young as Canada, just as conscious of superior health and morals, just as provincial, and just as ambitious to avoid those sewers.

I feel completely at home in the Canadian literary climate, even when its winds get shrill. I could be enlisted as a BB-caliber cultural Lafayette. Nothing in New York or Detroit, or for that matter in Mississippi, tells me anything about my own identity or my roots. As I said in *Wolf Willow*, I came back to Saskatchewan looking for those roots; and what Saskatchewan did not put into me, Montana and Utah and California did. I am content to have my world citizenship rooted in the West, though I don't want to be just a regionalist—and I will now risk outraging some of you by saying that it doesn't much matter whether the West means Canadian or American. I don't see much difference.

Identity, the truest sense of self and tribe, the deepest loyalty to place and way of life, is inescapably local, and it is my faith that all the most serious art and literature come out of that seedbed, even though the writer's experience goes far beyond it. Much of the felt life and the observed character and place that give a novel body and authenticity, much of the unconsciously absorbed store of images and ideas, comes ultimately from the shared experience of a community or region. There is a kind of provincialism, minus the aggressiveness and self-consciousness, that encompasses the most profound things that a writer has to say. Like civilizations, communities and regions have a youth, a maturity, an old age, perhaps a senile old age. The ones I am talking about are the nascent ones of the New World. It is the sense that they are so far unsaid, that something personal to one's self and one's tribe remains uncommunicated, that drives

some of us to write. And I submit that that has little to do
with nationality, and certainly with national*ism*, when we are
talking about the United States or Canada.

I know about the Innis theory of east-west force in Canada,
and about Professor Creighton's metropolitan circles of influence, and I grant validity to both. I know how indignant
Canadians can get when one brings up, as they say, that old
"north-south boundary line business." Nevertheless I am sure
that the logger in British Columbia *does* have more in common
with his counterpart in Washington than he does with somebody from Ontario. I am even more sure that the Saskatchewan wheat farmer shares more, in experience, climate, geography, occupational habit, folklore, language, vision, with the
other farmers down the long sweep of short-grass country that
runs from the North Saskatchewan to the Staked Plains, than
he does with an Ontario farmer. I have heard, and I tend to believe it, that the Maritimes flow more naturally into New England, the "Boston States," than into other parts of Canada, no
matter how strongly the fur trade and the railroads have
directed the consolidation of Canada east and west.

I am not now speaking of either economics or politics. I will
applaud when Canada frees itself from too much American
domination of its resource development, and I will be very de-
pressed if Canada or any segment of it breaks off to try secession
or annexation with the United States. I am talking about culture, way of life, shared experience, and recognitions. No *cor-
don sanitaire*, no nationalist fervor, is going to prevent that
kind of rapport between Canadians and Americans where great
geographical and climatic regions happen to slop over the
forty-ninth parallel. Whether patriots of either side like it or
not, we are one heterogeneous people sharing a continent. Historically, the sections have been far more important than social
and economic class in the United States. I think in the long
haul they may be more important than nationality, too, at least
in places, and sometimes more important even than race and
color.

And that, I know, calls for very hasty explanation, and the
explanation involves the observed or probable results of the

melting pot on the one hand and the cultural mosaic on the other.

Officially and unofficially, the United States has tried to Americanize all its various peoples for two hundred years. In theory an egalitarian democracy, it aroused in Tocqueville and others those fears of stereotype and mediocrity of which I spoke earlier. But is it a truly homogenized society, as George Grant and some others declare? On the contrary. Except briefly during two wars, it has never been a nation. It is the most incredible mixture of races, colors, political and religious and economic faiths, regions and subregions, Establishment and counterculture, highbrow, middlebrow, and lowbrow, conservative and revolutionary, in the entire round world. The melting pot has not melted Americans down; the mass media have not homogenized more than their surface.

Working against the forces of homogenization has been a certain American genius for refractoriness, rebellion, lawlessness, and change, which uncorrected can lead and has led to near anarchy. Americans are close to an ethnic slumgullion. There is, I suppose, a sort of standard American language, but it is subverted by pockets of stubbornly preserved dialect as well as by dialects that are in process of development out of the standard tongue, and this in spite of radio and television. Black English, to take one example, is close to unintelligible except to those who speak it.

Similarly, the regions, which ought to be flattened out into uniformity according to the theory, remain differentiated and even grow farther apart, and they even put their mark on people whom race and religion would seem to dominate. Ralph Ellison, for one example, is a very different type, with different speech and different reactions, from the usual black writer. He grew up neither in the South nor in a northern ghetto, but in the West.

Despite the flattening and leveling tendencies of the mass culture and despite the temptations to ethnic or cultural militancy and separatism and despite modern communication, the regions do, within broad limits, produce cultures and types that develop and maintain their own integrity. Between that sort of individuation and the more hectic sort promoted by ethnic groups, America has become something very different from the vulgar monolith its critics fear or despise. In the deeper levels of culture, the great monolithic neon-lighted barbarity is a bugaboo, a myth. The melting pot has been a bust.

But I wonder if the cultural mosaic won't be a partial bust too. Québec, again, I exempt; it is already culturally distinct and, beyond much doubt, will remain so indefinitely. But I wonder if the so-called ethnic cultures will persist for more than a generation or two in the free society of Canada. The way to make immigrant or native cultures persist is to persecute and oppress them, as the United States has oppressed the Blacks, Chicanos, Indians, Orientals, and others who now revive secessionism in ethnic and cultural terms a hundred years after the Civil War disposed of secessionism as a regional and political philosophy. Leave them free, in a predominantly English-speaking country, and they will pretty surely become Canadians, English-speaking, with perhaps residual cultural attachments such as religion and some trimmings like *Fastnachtkuchen* or *fattigmand* at Christmas, plus some contributions that have gone toward the alteration, or creation, of the Canadian image.

It seems to me a significant irony that the melting pot, which was meant to produce uniformity and a national character, produced instead diversity and half a hundred regional or ethnic characters with only broad resemblances. It would be a comparable irony if the mosaic theory, meant to retain diversity, should produce more uniformity than most people expect. I think it will. I also think, and have said, that the uniformities will exist ultimately, if they don't already, within a regional diversity. And that is the pattern which the United States seems to me to be reaching by the opposite route.

I doubt that when William Kurelek painted the pictures that illustrate his *A Prairie Boy's Winter* he was being either self-consciously Canadian or self-consciously Ukrainian. He was painting out of his memory of indelible childhood experience, and his memory is beautifully and evocatively regional. Those pictures speak to me like trumpets, they are full of instant recognitions, they remind me at every turn of the page of things I have not forgotten but only mislaid. They do in paint what I tried only half successfully to do in words in *Wolf Willow.* I guarantee they will speak with great force to anyone, of any ethnic background, who grew up in short-grass country, on the plains, whether those plains are north of the forty-ninth parallel or south of it. I'd like to try them on George McGovern and see if they don't say to him, like church bells, SOUTH DA-KOTA! But I know they are not going to speak with quite that force to someone from British Columbia, where the physical bases of life are different.

A hundred years and more after the search for an American identity began, William Dean Howells advised his country's writers to be as American as they unconsciously could. That advice comes close to Robinson Jeffers's dream of being passionately at peace, but it will probably have to do. A Canadian literature as Canadian as it can unconsciously be will depend on what such things always depend on: on the perceptiveness, passion, and integrity of individual writers and the eloquence with which they make their own lives and the lives of their tribe meaningful to the world. There is nothing wrong with Canadian literature that one or two world-class writers wouldn't cure. They will happen. The nationalistic debates of the Connecticut Wits led by a crooked but sure path to *Huckleberry Finn.*

The West Coast:
Region with a View

During the last two days of October, there gathered at the Highlands Inn, in Carmel, California, one of those conferences that are periodic within the learned professions. The subject, "Has the West Coast an Identifiable Culture?" was calculated to permit the discussion of everything from piety and local prejudice to statistical social analysis. The conferees included four historians, three professors of English, two anthropologists, a philosopher, a college president, a college chaplain, a professor of music, a sociologist, the director of an art museum, the director of the California Department of Beaches and Parks, the director of a university press, the editor of the West's most successful magazine, a music and art critic, an architectural writer, the San Francisco *Time* man, a distinguished architect, two novelists, and the vice-president of the American Council of Learned Societies, which was picking up the check.

Into this pleasant two-day conversation the term "regionalism" was introduced early. The terms of the conference seemed to force us toward the sin of cultural narcissism. What we decided (and it could be nothing very precise, because it was immediately clear to all of us that the region had had no such adequate studies as make generalization possible in some other regions, and was in such a state of flux that it was not likely to have any for a considerable time) is not my subject here. I was more interested in something else revealed by the talks: that among those twenty-five people there was not a single serious defender of the kind of regionalism that used to be argued, and sometimes chanted, during the years when I was growing up in the Rocky Mountains, an immature region, and the Midwest, a somewhat more developed one.

The self-conscious zeal and the mystique were missing at Carmel. Nobody much cared whether the West Coast was called one region or three: Clearly it was either or both. Nobody much cared whether the architecture, music, painting, and literature of the Coast were mystically indigenous or not; nobody felt that it was vital for him to concern himself intensively with local themes, settings, characters, and "spirit." More important than those questions of idiosyncrasy in the local arts were the questions "How lively is any of these arts, as measured by both its local and its national or international acceptance?" and "How good is it?" And that is a big change from the organic theory of inevitable cultural maturation that most Americans have accepted, passively or aggressively, for more than a hundred years. By the organic theory, localism and virtue are all but synonymous.

I was not surprised to see regionalism in decline—it has been in decline in every region except in the rear-guard South for years. But I was surprised to see it in nearly total eclipse, especially on the West Coast, where the boom has forced an extreme self-awareness, and most especially in a conference which invited all the traditional responses.

We have always, as a civilization, been compelled to periodic examinations and self-appraisals. Trying to establish who we were—or that we really were somebody—we have smarted under the criticism of British travelers, and have pondered Tocqueville and Lord Bryce, and studied how imported institutions, habits, arts, and ways of thinking adapt themselves on a new continent or in new regions of the continent, and how (this is often pure hope) they become something new and (this is piety) better. Self-discovery has been our need and our theme. Patriotism and the organic theory were twin-born yokels. The critic who remarked back in Jefferson's time that "the chorus of every play is in the hearts of the audience" was implying an intimate bond between small-c culture and large-C Culture, between the society and the arts which expressed it. He did not say, though he might have, Mature the society and the arts will follow as the day the night, and they will echo in the hearts of the audience, because it is of and by and from the people that the matured cultural voice speaks.

Emerson and Whitman would say that for him later on. The Emerson who got tired of the courtly muses of Europe and celebrated the native and the low was at once acknowledging a historical trend and asserting a new value. The Whitman who visioned democratic archetypes and foreheard voices that spoke for a whole people was formulating doctrine that seventy or eighty years later consoled Iowa poets yearning for the slow Midland earth to get on with its essential production of a small-c culture so that they could speak with its voice. Ellis Parker Butler's motto for Iowa, "Ten million yearly for manure but not one cent for literature," would not indefinitely apply. Wait, only wait, and mature your powers. Like Marxism, a local literature was organic and inevitable. Like the classless society, it would come.

The organic theory was essential to the self-respect of us colonials and provincials. It gave us a critical touchstone and the beginnings of a literary history; our jobs were to evaluate local writings in terms of the organic expectations and to hang those which passed the test, like Christmas-tree balls, on the skimpy tree of the local tradition. The organic theory could be used as well in promoting Chicago against Boston, or Nashville or Iowa City against New York, as in asserting America against courtly Europe. When the national literature broke into sections after the Civil War, the organic theory broke with it. Eventually it took over, informed, and enlarged the local-color movement, purged its excesses, gave it a common doctrine, and set about replacing the tourist writers of local color with the Whitmanesque voices of local culture. The Great American

Novel was now to come not single and whole from the nation but piecemeal from the regions.

William Dean Howells, in wanting American writers to be as American as they unconsciously could, admitted the self-consciousness of the movement he had steered for many years. He meant that the best writers grow as naturally as apples on a tree, the way he had grown in Ohio and Mark Twain in Missouri. When it happened according to the organic inevitabilities, nationalism or regionalism provided the highest kind of art, and locals were its best judges, as boys and blackbirds were the best judges of berry patches.

That was the doctrine I grew up on, and to a point I will still defend it. It has demonstrably worked, in region after region. Given the proper conditions, it will always work. But the proper conditions involve a relative homogeneity of life in relative isolation over a relatively long period, and that combination is increasingly hard to find. The national character as demonstrated by a Lincoln or analyzed by a Howells or Twain or James was being lost in the rush even while we thought we recognized his face. Industrialism was drumming him under, immigrations of a hundred nationalities and religions and cultural traditions were sweeping him away. Except in rural areas, especially the South, where isolation has not been broken down and the local patterns have remained nearly intact, regionalism has pretty well gone, and the organic theory, if not discredited, is indefinitely suspended in the face of incessant larger syntheses. So what we used to believe expressed a region has turned out, often, to express no more than a period. In the longer view, it looks not like a consummation but like a phase.

Obviously neither the West Coast nor any of its three subregions has a regional culture or regional arts in the traditional terms. For one thing, no part of it has really matured in isolation. Even the Northwest, relatively homogeneous and relatively the most isolated, has been a door to Alaska and a window on Asia, and it is primarily in its woods and its cow country, its James Stephenses and H. L. Davises, that it has developed a regional strain of literature. And what of those novels of rural California that Hamlin Garland foresaw, what of those

sunny lads and lasses—or maidens—working and loving under
the palms? Well, California agriculture began with cattle,
shifted to wheat, developed water and shifted again to truck
crops, rice, cotton, fruit. But it never had as its basis that
160-acre yeoman that the American gospels, and Garland with
them, assumed. It has always been factories in the field. Jump
from *Ramona* to *The Octopus* to *The Grapes of Wrath* and
discover how discontinuous and broken is the California agricultural environment and how persistent is the "largeness" of
the operations. Cattle persist, and cowboys, but go up into the
foothills and meet them. They are largely second- and third-
generation Italians. Not even in the rural areas is there a continuity even of ethnic stocks.

The West Coast, California especially, is actually profoundly
nonrural. California's 80 percent urbanization matches that of
the Middle Atlantic States. It is not inhabited by quaint provincials, and never was. San Francisco in particular has always
been a city of an unsurpassed worldliness, a city of sin and excitement and gold. Not only was California a more persuasive
image of the earthly paradise than Kansas or Dakota prairie
land, but it demanded initiative and some capital to get there,
and something like selective immigration took place. Though it
drew people of every kind and class, it drew a relatively higher
proportion of the educated and cultivated than did other parts
of the West; and it drew them, in one of the most remarkable
movements of population in recent times, from all over the
world.

The advantages that San Francisco enjoyed were enjoyed in
somewhat less lavishness by both the Northwest and the Los
Angeles area. The setting of both is spectacular, the climate of
both is mild. Los Angeles began its boom with a railroad price
war and one-dollar tickets to the Pacific, and has mushroomed
ever since on sunshine, oranges, oil, Hollywood, and airplanes.
But it, too, has drawn heavily from the ranks of writers and artists and musicians, and it, too, if only because of its styles and
its movie and television industries, is a variety of world city. So
is Seattle. So is Portland. No isolation in any of them, and no
homogeneity, and no holding still. To make social studies of

any of those cities would be like trying to hold a stethoscope to
the chest of an angry cat. And hence no traditional regionalism; perhaps no identifiable West Coast culture.

Quite obviously the twenty-five men sitting around a table in
Carmel had much in common. They all lived in places strongly
on the boom, places that multitudes of people move into but
that few people ever move out of. They all shared a peculiarly
West Coast view of the Pacific and of Asia, a degree of famili-
arity and awareness created entirely by propinquity. They
shared big agriculture and except for the coastal strip from
about Eureka, California, northward they shared a water shortage. Very largely, the West Coast, like all the rest of the Far
West, is an oasis civilization. They shared a style of domestic
architecture that more than any other single cultural manifes-
tation deserves to be called regional in the old sense and that is
probably imported more enthusiastically into other regions
than any other West Coast product. They shared colossal head-
aches incident upon explosive growth, lack of planning, com-
mercialism, and public apathy: overcrowded highways, double-
session schools, housing developments that at their cheapest
and worst are about as aesthetic and as socially healthful as
ringworm. They acknowledged for their own subregions a bad
case of togetherness and conformity, possibly brought on by
the need of new immigrants to root themselves, conform, belong. They shared an anxiety probably more acute than that of
the country at large, if religious cultism, a marked growth in
the more conservative denominations, very high suicide and alcoholism rates, and a vast yeasty ferment of amateur creative-
ness may all be lumped together as indications of social unease.

Eagerness to conform and belong may in themselves be
causes of anxiety when it is not clear what one can or should
conform to. By the evidence of both the editor of *Sunset* and
the director of the California Beaches and Parks, one common
way is to seize upon the natural environment, make greedy use
of the parks, forests, beaches, campsites, make a fetish of the
barbecue and barbecue weather. Precisely because there are so
many new migrants, most of them eagle-eyed for the patterns
to which they ought to conform, the West Coast as a region

shows a blurred image. No group, even an intimate group in one of the subregions, could sit down and find in common such things as the *Fugitive* group in Nashville found: a common agrarian tradition with a philosophy to match, a common Protestantism lit by revivalism, a common racial and cultural background, a common lost cause, a common hatred, a common guilt.

On the West Coast, no such unanimity of tradition and belief. No voices, no archetypes, no Great Pacific Slope Novel. And yet, from Seattle to San Diego a tremendous stir, a great swell of energy and optimism and creativity, and this may be the truest, though not necessarily the most traditional, expression of a really regional spirit. For the ferment is not simply economic, not just a building boom and the skyrocketing of the electronics and aircraft and missile industries. This society—urban, opulent, anxious, energetic, highly unionized, with a per-capita income exceeded by that of only four or five states, growing at a furious rate, situated in a region whose climate is on the whole more beatific and whose natural setting is more spectacular than those of any other section—this society is not sitting on its hands or relapsing into Spanish-Californian somnolence. In spite of the sports cars and the Rolls-Royces (thirteen of the forty U.S. Rolls-Royce agencies are in California), and in spite of the swimming pools and the homes that cost two, three, four hundred thousand dollars, this society strains for something more. Perhaps it is uneasily asking itself Max Lerner's question "After prosperity, what?" Perhaps it is conforming, or trying to conform, to some regional image of creativity, as my Norwegian grandparents consciously tried to conform to the outlines of midwestern character.

In any case there is a curious ambivalence detectable—or at least I seemed to detect it in the findings of the Carmel conference. For along with the uneasiness, the anxiety, the uncertainty and fumbling for identification, there is in the whole West Coast, and there was among the twenty-five conferees at Carmel, a confidence so sublime that it is hardly even conscious of itself. By the end of the meeting, we were assuring ourselves that it would be totally false to try to justify or even identify West Coast culture in organic or regional terms. Never having felt isolated or provincial or inferior, the Coast doesn't have to wedge itself forward.

Two days at Carmel convinced most of us that we felt pretty much like the rest of the United States, only more so. Our language is a representative amalgam almost undistinguished by local dialectal peculiarities; ethnically we are more mixed even than the eastern seaboard cities; in a prosperous country, we are more prosperous than most; in an urban country, more urban than most; in a gadget-happy country, more addicted to gadgets; in a mobile country, more mobile; in a tasteless country, more tasteless; in a creative country, more energetically creative; in an optimistic society, more optimistic; in an anxious society, more anxious.

Contribute regionally to the national culture? We *are* the national culture, at its most energetic end.

It is exhilarating when twenty-five intelligent and articulate people discover at the same time that they share so egregious and brash a confidence. Newcomer or native son, we all had it. We asked ourselves what was most characteristic about the architecture which was the Coast's most distinctive regional contribution, and we found that it was open, outward-turning, the reverse of the inward-turning and cavelike and protective. We looked out the windows down at the headland of Point Lobos, where land and water and sun met magnificently, and we knew one of the reasons people came—we among them—and seldom left. We began to add up the signs of cultural life, all the way from the San Francisco opera season and the somewhat magniloquent Hollywood Bowl to the unsponsored and spontaneous creative cutting edges: the jazz renaissance in San Francisco, the weekly theater on the campus of the University of Washington, the centers of poetry and fiction, the new patterns of neighborhood theater and neighborhood music in the sprawling noncity of Los Angeles, the art museums, the galleries, the painters of the so-called San Francisco School, who would actually be quite as much at home almost anywhere since most of them are abstract expressionists. We counted Nobel Prize winners in West Coast universities and the people we knew who had recently been filched by West Coast schools from the Ivy League, and artists, writers, musicians, painters, who had chosen to be born here or to come here. For a little while we were like a delighted bunch of regional patriots counting our successes—except that there was practically nothing of traditional regionalism in us. Half of the people we cited as signs of great creative growth were in-migrants, as were half of ourselves. That was no problem. That was precisely how the rest of the country and the rest of the world *did* contribute to us; that was simply greater evidence of centrality.

Robert Frost, whom if I were a regionalist I would instantly identify as having been born in San Francisco, had a test by which he judged a man: How well can he swing what he knows? The West Coast beyond question can afford to know more, but what it knows it can swing. It thinks it can swing the whole country. If I ever saw a region that feels its oats, this is it.

From its great eyes on Mount Palomar, Mount Wilson, Mount Hamilton, the West Coast looks farther into space than anyone anywhere. That is something to fasten upon. But take another symbol. On the grand prow of land above the Golden Gate, looking north across the soar and lift of the bridge to the Marin hills, and eastward across San Francisco's roofs and streets, and westward toward the last promontory below which the Pacific spreads vast and blue, sits one of San Francisco's three art museums, the Palace of the Legion of Honor. It is formally French, a replica. The late William Wurster, the dean of Bay Area architects as well as of the University of California School of Architecture, called it "the most inward-turning building upon the most outward-turning site in the world."

That building represents an old way of thinking; it demonstrates in a way the earliest, imitative, transplanted stage of the organic process. It is not likely that it or the spirit that produced it will have much influence on the future. For nothing else in this West Coast amalgam is inward-turning. America at its farthest West and its highest voltage, it is a region, if it can be called a region at all, with a view. Like lemmings, the nation has beaten its way to the western edge and the last sunsets on the continent, but only a few jump off the Golden Gate in frustration at having nowhere else to go. The rest of them are busy preparing the coast as a launching platform for the future.

I believe this truly is not a region but the mainstream, America only more so. Both the good and the bad are more so. Sight of what some builders have been permitted to do along the Skyline road south of San Francisco would bring tears to the eyes of a hangman. The North Beach bohemia that for some reason seemed to represent San Francisco to the world for a season was a dreary borrowing, an inward-turning if there ever was one, a death wish in a crying towel. Much of this, and much of every hideousness of our automotive civilization. And yet what a surge, how much life, how much exuberant and not always controlled power—above all, what confidence! The West Coast has the calm confidence of a Christian with four aces, and Mark Twain, who knew it in its earlier exuberance, would be the first to say so. If Lerner's "After prosperity, what?" is an answerable question, the West Coast is going to have a good deal to do about framing the answer.

Making a Myth

Few books provide their readers with ringside seats for the conception and birth of a demigod. *My Dear Wister* does. In its pages we watch the complete, triumphant ontogeny of the cowboy hero, the most imagination-catching and durable of our mythic figures. Owen Wister and Frederic Remington, whose collaboration is the subject of Ben Vorpahl's study, create him before our eyes. They begin to mold him out of the observed realities of the brief, furious, passing empire of the cattlemen. They shape him by imitation and trial and error into the hero of a romantic fiction, and in the process they are themselves shaped, as the cowboy image is, by the torque of an anonymous, public, everywhere-and-nowhere myth-making impulse. Believing they record reality, they helplessly remake it larger than life, until when they are done their creation rides off the page into the sunset of a thousand horse operas, the free, lonely, self-reliant, skilled, eternally ambiguous embodiment of a national, indeed a human, fantasy.

In this mythifying process, Mr. Vorpahl makes clear, Owen Wister had a larger part than Remington. The writer was tuned in to literary and historical wavelengths that, at least at first, made no sound on the artist's receiver. Remington, active, restless, aggressive, ironic, as romantic as Wister but in less literary ways, was primarily an eye, a quick, accurate, unsentimental eye, and a hand that could record swiftly what the eye saw.

Temperamentally he was closer to such a realistic reporter as Andy Adams than he was to Wister. Not in the least a prettifier, an idealizer, or a theorizer, he saw particulars, he noted details, he recorded the thousand quick glints of the western life that fascinated him. The complaint of E. Douglas Branch, that *The Virginian* contains not one scene of cowboys working with cattle, could not be made against the drawings of Remington. He swarms with scenes of an indescribable variety, all explosive with action either kinetic or potential: cowboys roping, cowboys branding, cowboys driving cattle, cowboys fighting Indians or each other, cowboys riding broncs, cowboys standing by a corral fence swapping horses. And every other sort of western picture: a cavalry troop in full charge, scouts bending intently over hostile tracks, Indians dragging a victim into the brush, packers tightening cinches, pack mules somersaulting over cliffs, squaws breaking camp, warriors encircling wagon trains. He was after the particulars. Wister, in the long run, was after a character type. Each of the collaborators affected the other, but it was Wister's more than Remington's imagination that produced the archetypal cowboy. Remington's sketches and paintings, intended as forthright recording or illustration, a report on reality, have tended to remain just that; but that still allows them to be subordinated to the Wister idea, and used as corroboration for the heightened cowboy of fantasy.

Wister made several tries, with results that satisfied him only partially, before he put together the Virginian after twenty years of effort. Lin McLean, Specimen Jones, and Scipio LeMoyne are all fumblings toward the character who, while still reflecting reality, would approximate the ideal figure that seems to have been persistently, if dimly, in Wister's mind. Because these early tries were outdone and obliterated by their triumphant successor, they have been pretty well forgotten, along with the Remington drawings that gave them visual reality. And perhaps because Remington did not illustrate *The Virginian*, the one Wister book that most moderns know, we have tended to forget how close the collaboration between them was, how intimate was the exchange of ideas and experiences, and how influential Remington was upon the creation we usually credit to Wister. This book reminds us of what we should not have forgotten, as it reminds us what a large part a third man, Theodore Roosevelt, had in popularizing the cowboy image.

That image, before Roosevelt, Remington, and Wister remade it, was hardly heroic or glamorous. As Henry Nash Smith points out in *Virgin Land*, the cowboy during his first decade was usually called a "herder," and through the 1870s he appeared in the public prints (and in at least one Presidential Message) as rough, shaggy, uncouth, barbarous, violent—at the very least a disturber of the peace and at the worst a brutal outlaw. He did not begin to take on the qualities of a hero until after the first Wild West Show, in North Platte, Nebraska, in 1882, when a cowboy named Buck Taylor attracted the attention of Prentiss Ingraham. Beginning in 1887, Ingraham immortalized this rodeo cowboy, first in a fictitious biography and then in a series of dime novels. He devised for him some colorful semi-Mexican garb that made him picturesque, and he endowed him with all the skill, courage, and masculine grace that have marked every heroic expression of the folk mind from Odysseus to Robin Hood, and from Leatherstocking to Superman.

By the time the cowboy thus made his way into literature— significantly through the basement door of the dime novels— the great drives that had produced him were over. The transcontinental railroad, which came into the West almost simultaneously with Texas cattle, left the open range split and exposed. The big die-up of the winter of 1886–87 had bankrupted many cattle outfits, altered the feudal conditions of range life, and made the cowboy less a knight-errant and more a hired man on horseback. By 1892, the year of Owen Wister's first two western stories, the Johnson County War had discredited the cattleman and his cowboy gun thugs in many eyes, and encouraged the Populism that Wister despised. Civilization, which both Wister and Remington saw as destructive to the West and its wild freedom, meant responsibility, meant law, meant fences and homesteads and water rights and fee-simple land ownership, meant women. It was inevitably on the side of the "nesters," whom Wister and his first Wyoming host, Major Wolcott, called "thieves" or "rustlers," and on whom Wolcott in fact, and the Virginian in fiction, visited vigilante law. By the time Wister began to know the West, the open range was already passing, and he acknowledged history in his novel by letting the Virginian take up land, marry, and settle down to the tamed routines of stock farming. After the last brief flare-up of youth, wildness, and killing, it is Molly Wood, and all she stands for, who wins.

But Molly Wood does not dominate the novel. "The heroine is the failure," Wister's acidulous mother wrote him. He admitted that she had no character, and he was right. She had not grown noticeably beyond the mining-camp schoolmarm bequeathed to him by Bret Harte. But the cowpuncher himself was another matter. He had engrossed all of Wister's attention, he was the reason for the novel's existence, and neither the end of the drives, nor the big die-up, nor the cattle wars, nor the fencing of the range, nor the coming of civilization affected the mythic horseman Wister created. The tame ending that Wister gave him does not, in fact, "take." In the reader's imagination the Virginian remains what he was before Molly threw a loop over him. He is as timeless and unchanging as Remington pictured him in "The Last Cavalier," and he is so because the national mythmaking urge that obscurely guided Wister's creation demanded that he be so.

This is no place to try to follow the wishful dream of which the Virginian is a late and very American embodiment, but one can suggest some of its forms. It is the dream of the Golden Age, the Earthly Paradise, and it is at least as old as Hesiod, who flourished in the eighth century B.C. It has as many variants as the religions with which it has often been associated, and depending on the status and condition of its dreamers it has been a resting place for heroes, a Valhalla or Elysium; it has been the place of lost perfection, the garden from which we have been expelled; it has been the many utopias toward which we yearn; it has been a belly-haven like Cockaigne or the Big Rock Candy Mountain or the railroaders' Indian Valley Line, where every day is payday. It has been the land of heart's desire, whatever that desire was, and so has taken forms that are political, social, religious, or simply plenteous.

Through the centuries, it has characteristically been located in the past, in the future, or in a faraway place difficult to reach. But with the discovery of America it became something suddenly possible; all the wishfulness of oppressed, hungry, restricted, ambitious mankind clustered on the new continent like flies on a wound. Every romantic hope of the Earthly Paradise, the perfect society, the New Jerusalem, found a home here. Attempts to establish them constitute a substantial part of our history. Sometimes the strength of the yearning and the persuasiveness of a tradition centuries old led actual travelers to see what was not there, as did William Bartram, whose reports of a Florida paradise bubbled up through Coleridge's opium dream and became the pleasure dome of Kubla Khan. Sometimes the unknown, with its unknown dangers, struck terror to men's hearts, as it did to the pilgrims on the *Mayflower*. Sometimes a great man could contemplate the New World as a little metaphor of the old one, complete with both good and evil, as Shakespeare did when he transformed a West Indies shipwreck island in *The Tempest*. But even there we see in Prospero a degree of power over the threats and conditions of life that is itself part of the dream, and will become increasingly a characteristic of the figures with whom the dream is peopled.

By and large, hopefulness has demonstrated itself a far stronger force in the American versions of the dream than either submission to evil or skepticism. Natural goodness, or the merely natural, has found a happier home in America than natural depravity; Ariel has outlasted Caliban. And it is a truism that the exploring and settling of a wilderness continent immensely increased, both in fact and in imagination, the freedom and self-reliance of a whole people. It was the baptism in wilderness that made the American a new man. Progressively westering frontiers encouraged and reinforced both the taste for total freedom and the expectation that it could be gratified. The contact with Indians, both as enemies and as models of savage liberty, was an incitement to primitivism. There were many more white men who went Indian than Indians who

went white. J. Hector St. John de Crèvecoeur, observing the
frontier from his safe and comfortable New York farm, was led
to speculate that much killing, and a steady diet of wild meat,
turned civilized men into solitaries and savages. In much the
same realistic spirit, Owen Wister after five years of experience
in the West concluded that "this negligent irresponsible wilderness tends to turn people shiftless, cruel, and incompetent."

Crèvecoeur would have been on the side of Molly Wood and
civilization; he would have found the Virginian's early life not
romantic but degrading. Yet it was Crèvecoeur who asked the
question that lay wordless beneath America's acute consciousness of itself: "Who is the American, this new man?"
Crèvecoeur answered the question in rational and optimistic
terms, citing wide-open opportunity, reward for hard work, social justice, political equality, religious freedom, self-respect,
and independence as some of the gifts of the New World to
the human condition. But others, less speculative and articulate
than Crèvecoeur, were already engaged in posing the question
by the lives they led, and answering it in a different way. *Letters from an American Farmer* was published in 1782. Seven
years earlier, Daniel Boone had led the first party of settlers
across the Cumberland Gap into Kentucky, and in 1784 John
Filson's *The Discovery, Settlement, and Present State of Ken-
tucke* launched Boone as a folk hero, the first of the great
American archetypes.

What Filson began, James Fenimore Cooper continued in
the Leatherstocking Tales, the first of which was published in
1823. Leatherstocking has come a long way from Hesiod's Age
of Heroes, and the American wilderness is not automatically
recognizable as one of the phases of the Golden Age. Nevertheless the connection is traceable, and has been traced: by
Howard Mumford Jones in *O Strange New World*, by Henry
Nash Smith in *Virgin Land*, by Perry Miller in *Errand into the
Wilderness*, by dozens more. Smith in particular follows the de-
scendants of Leatherstocking in their several shapes as woods-
men, rivermen, mountain men, cowboys, dime-novel heroes,
and badmen. He notes the places and times where the original
Leatherstocking persona, at first low-caste and hence not a suit-

able husband for a romantic heroine, divided in two and added to his first function as frontier expert, protector, and right-hand man the further functions of a romantic lead, as in *The Virginian*. In the nearly eighty years between Cooper's *The Pioneers* and *The Virginian*, the mythic figure was democratized, or the story around him was. If Wister had been writing *The Virginian* in the 1820s, his dude, modeled upon his well-born self, would have had to marry Molly Wood, and the Virginian would have had to ride on into the sunset.

The fact that the cowboy hero does marry the heroine, and does not ride on into the sunset, is actually, as I have been suggesting, the element of the story in which factual reporting clashes with myth. Wister's cowboy is a little too close to history at the end. If he had been purified one stage further, as he has been in numerous horse operas since, he would look more like Leatherstocking—rootless, homeless, an orphan, an eternal wanderer, a celibate, and as D. H. Lawrence took pains to point out, a chronic killer. Shane.

Wister himself half recognized what his romantic love story was doing to his mythical discovery or creation of the cowboy character. He knew that the cowboy West was a predominantly masculine fact, and he half comprehended that it was also a predominantly masculine dream. In the article "The Evolution of the Cowpuncher," which as Mr. Vorpahl demonstrates is a key document in the collaboration between Wister and Remington, Wister remarks on what almost every student of the cowboy and cowboy literature has observed: his curious indifference to women. "No soldier of fortune ever adventured with bolder carelessness, no fiercer blood ever stained a border. War they made in plenty, but not love; for the woman they saw was not the woman a man can take into his heart."

In that last clause I believe he sins not only against historical fact—for in fact plenty of cowpunchers did take into their hearts, when their time came, the sort of women who were available—but in his interpretation. It was not a shortage of women, or women of the right kind, that kept the cowpuncher a bachelor. It was the compulsion of the dream, which was a masculine dream of action, adventure, and danger, a hero's dream that is still potent with millions of movie and TV watchers. Women are a threat to that dream, more dangerous to male freedom than Comanches or Apaches or rival gunfighters. And that, too, has its roots deep in a tradition centuries old. It is only the Mohammedans who have made woman one of the delights of the paradise dream. As Frank E. and Fritzie P. Manuel point out in "The History of Paradise," "In the West paradise and sexual love have rarely coexisted."

It was Crèvecoeur's question that Wister set out to answer, but his answer was hurried by the swiftness with which the West changed, and it incorporated incompatible elements from the mythic, which controlled Wister, and the actual, which had considerable diversionary influence on Wister and dominated Remington. From the moment when he decided to become the cowboy's chronicler, incompatible impulses were at work in him. In a much-quoted passage from *Roosevelt: The Story of a Friendship*, he reports the moment of decision. "Why wasn't some Kipling saving the sagebrush for American literature, before the sagebrush and all that it signified went the way of the California forty-niner . . . ? Roosevelt had seen the sagebrush true, had felt its poetry, and also Remington, who illustrated his articles so well. But what was fiction doing, fiction, the only thing that has always outlived fact?"

So he set out, as Remington did, to preserve and record the facts of range life. But he wanted to do it in fiction, which outlives fact. The contradiction was never fully resolved. Remington's influence was heavily on the side of the actual. It is clear that in urging Wister to write "The Evolution of the Cowpuncher" he had in mind something far different from the kind of chivalric lineage from feudal knights in armor that Wister produced. But Wister, though he enjoyed and carefully recorded western life through many summers, felt from the beginning an urge to define and comprehend a new culture and a new culture hero, and believed that in doing so he would define the essential American. In a way, he did, but it was not by way of the notebook that he did it. It was from the seed of fantasy and myth that the Virginian grew. He existed in Wister's mind as a seed before Wister ever saw Wyoming.

What he saw there, and what Remington taught him, was documentation, corroboration. As he said of Corporal Skirdin, whose practical joke he wrote into Chapter Three, he was not a *source* of the Virginian. He was "a sort of incarnation. . . . He ratified my imagination."

How imagination was ratified is the subject of *My Dear Wister*. It is a fascinating study in how myth and fact interweave to form the incarnate fantasies that we call culture heroes.

A. B. Guthrie

A. B. Guthrie's *The Big Sky* does not belie its title. It is a novel lived entirely in the open. The big wild places are both its setting and its theme, and everything about the book is as big as the country it moves in. The story sweeps westward from Kentucky to St. Louis and up the interminable Missouri through Omaha and Pawnee country, past Ree and Sioux country, into Stoney and Big Belly and Blackfoot country, and there, riding on the boil of its own excitement, it waits out its climax. Bigness, distance, wildness, freedom are the dream that pulls Boone Caudill westward into the mountains, and the dream has an incandescence in the novel because it is also the dream that Bud Guthrie grew up on.

The country he takes us through with Caudill, Jim Deakins, and Dick Summers is his native landscape, known since childhood. It is a sign of commitment, an evidence of love, that when he gives wildness its fleeting consummation by settling Boone Caudill in a Blackfoot lodge with the girl Teal Eye, he locates that idyllic camp on the river called variously the Tansy, Breast, Teton, or Titty—essentially the valley around Choteau, Montana, where Guthrie lived as a boy and has settled as a man. It is country of a kind I know well—at the edge of the mountains but not in them: high plains country, chinook country, its air like a blade or a blowtorch, its sky fitting down close and tight to the horizon and the great bell of heaven alive with light, clouds, heat, stars, winds, incomparable weathers. But even if I had never been within a thousand miles of Montana I could not miss Guthrie's love and knowledge of the land he writes about, and I could not avoid knowing something of what that unmarked wilderness would have meant to a Boone Caudill. The big plains and the surging ranges and the hidden valleys are a fit setting for his story of intractable liberty and violence; and in the end they turn out to be not only a setting and a theme but also, like Caudill himself, victim. The West of *The Big Sky* is innocence, anticivilization, savage and beautiful and doomed, a dream that most Americans, however briefly or vainly, have dreamed, and that some have briefly captured.

Serious writers about the West have often had to celebrate scenery for lack of the social complexities out of which most fiction is made. Geography, at least, is one matter in which a Westerner can excel and in which he takes pride. History is another. For in a region only three generations from the total wilderness of buffalo and horse Indians, everything, including history, must be built from scratch. Like any other part of the human tradition, history is an artifact. It does not exist until it is remembered and written down; and it is not truly remembered and written down until it has been vividly imagined. We become our past, and it becomes a part of us, by our reliving of our beginnings. Guthrie's first three novels, which form a loose trilogy, have as one of their justifications the creation of such a usable human memory. They are focused on Guthrie's home country, but they have validity for the entire West.

These are novels, works of the imagination, and yet it is not improper to think of them as related to the trilogy of great histories that constitute the major work of Guthrie's friend Bernard DeVoto. DeVoto touched history with a novelist's imagination; Guthrie imagines his novels around a historian's sure knowledge. These two, each after his own impressions, together took the long journey up the Missouri in the wake of the fur hunters' keelboats, and their imaginative reconstructions cover much common ground. *The Big Sky*, a story of mountain men, pairs off naturally with *Across the Wide Mis-*

souri; *The Way West*, chronicling the trail to Oregon, goes in team with *The Year of Decision, 1846*. But that is as far as the parallel extends. DeVoto goes backward, gathering up all the history of western exploration in *The Course of Empire*, while Guthrie goes onward in time to deal, in *These Thousand Hills*, with the Montana cattle empire of the 1880s.

Nevertheless, the man from Utah and the man from Montana share a characteristic western impulse. They are intent on creating a past, firming up a ground on which the present can stand and by which it can be comprehended. And both make whatever use can be made of those slight, accidental linkages by which discrete happenings become historical continuity. Thus, Guthrie, completely in accordance with historical probability, returns Dick Summers to the wild country of his youth as guide to an Oregon train in *The Way West*; and again in accordance with probability, has Lat Evans, son of Brownie and Mercy Evans of *The Way West*, trail a herd of Durham cattle eastward from Oregon into Montana in *These Thousand Hills*. And when Lat Evans stakes out his own ranch after a career of wolfing and bronc busting, he stakes it out on the same Tansy, Breast, Teton, or Titty River where Boone Caudill had lived his idyll with Teal Eye and the Piegans of Heavy Runner's band—and where later a boy named Bud Guthrie, son of the editor of the Choteau *Acantha*, would be hanging out his ears listening to cowpunchers, sheepherders, drifters, politicians, and wandering journalists talking of a past that no one yet had begun to write down.

The Big Sky is the first, and for me the best, of the three novels that eventually came of that listening. What makes it special is not merely its narrative and scenic vividness, but the ways in which Boone Caudill exemplifies and modifies an enduring American type.

Caudill is an avatar of the oldest of all the American myths: the civilized man re-created in savagery, rebaptized into innocence on a wilderness continent. His fabulous ancestors are Daniel Boone, who gives him his name, and Cooper's Leatherstocking; and up and down the range of American fiction he has ten thousand recognizable sibs. But Caudill has his own

distinction, for he is neither intellectualized nor senti-
mentalized. He may be White Indian, but he is no Noble
Savage—for the latter role he is not noble enough, and far too
savage. Though he retains many mythic qualities—the preter-
natural strength and cunning, the need for wild freedom, the
larger-than-life combination of Indian skills and white mind—
he has no trace of Leatherstocking's deist piety. His virtues are
stringently limited to the qualities of self-reliance, courage,
and ruthlessness that will help him to survive a life in which
few die old. Guthrie clearly admires him, though with reserva-
tions enforced by the hindsights of history. Boone Caudill's
savagery, admirable and even enviable though it is, can lead nowhere. The moral of his lapse from civilization is that such an
absolute lapse is doomed and sterile, and in the end the savagery which has been his strength is revealed as his fatal weakness.

For Boone's course leaves him nowhere to go. By mid-novel,
having fled the settlements' law and the authority of a harsh father, he has cut himself off so utterly that he can hardly stand
the civilization of so remote an outpost as Fort Union, on the
Yellowstone. He elects the wild, he symbolically marries the
wilderness when he brings Teal Eye into his tepee on the
Teton. But that, too, the one thing he wants, the one thing he
is fit for, will be his only a little while. He is a killing machine,
as dangerous to what he loves as to what he hates, and what
the logic of his ferocious adaptation demands, the novel's action fulfills. In the same moment when he shoots Jim Deakins,
the one friend who has bound him to the past and to civilization, he breaks his bond with Teal Eye and the Blackfeet;
and the son who might have represented continuity and a compromise between the two ways of life has been—how properly
for both the historical rightness and the fictional inevitability
of his theme!—born blind.

No compromise is possible for one who, like Boone Caudill,
has given himself all the way to savagery. He cannot go to
farming, as Dick Summers does, and he would be too intractable ever to lead out a wagon train to Oregon. As Fenimore
Cooper realized as early as *The Pioneers,* in 1823, the true

White Indian, whether woodsman or plainsman or mountain man, is doomed. Caudill is as incapable as Leatherstocking of becoming a venerable relic in a tamed community, but neither does Guthrie apotheosize him as a mythic Untamable facing into a western sunset and uttering a firm "Here!" in response to the ultimate Voice. Boone's end is less literary. Gloomy and guilt-ridden, possessing neither the security of the settlements nor the animal contentment of the wild, he simply fades out, disappears. It is not he, but the gentler Dick Summers, the white man who has adopted Indian ways without ceasing to be white man, who serves as the link between the world of beaver and the world of the western wagons.

This is to say that while Boone reveals all the large outlines of the myth, he retains a degree of realism, a marked quality of harshness and violence. In his temperament—which is what Guthrie added to the myth to create him—he is less like the standard frontier leading man than like the degenerated border type that in reality created and populated the frontier, the men whom Hector St. John de Crèvecoeur described as early as 1782: men "no better than carnivorous animals of a superior rank . . . dependent on their native tempers, and . . . remote from the power of example, and check of shame." "Once hunters," cried Crèvecoeur in a tone between philosophical disapproval and personal disgust, "farewell to the plough. The chase renders them ferocious, gloomy, and unsociable. . . . Eating of wild meat, whatever you may think, tends to alter their temper."

Ferocious, gloomy, and unsociable, de-civilized by the eating of wild meat. Boone Caudill might almost be a gloss on Crèvecoeur's observation. But it is his special excellence that he is something more. He is both mountain man and myth, both individual and archetype, which means that the record of his violent life is both credible and exhilarating. And he has one tender and attractive thing about him: an inarticulate but powerful love for the sweep of plain and peak and sky, the intimacy of cutbank and wild-rose island, the free distance shaped by butte and hogback and aspen-blotched mountainside. It is the thing he most clearly shares with his creator, the thing that can make a taciturn, bloodthirsty, unwashed, gut-eating white savage a character whom we follow with excitement and often with acute sympathy. For this part of him we share too, and we grant, if we are honest, that the dream of primitive innocence is likewise, and simultaneously, a dream of violence and unrestraint. However inappropriate to the civilization with which we have infected Boone Caudill's mountains, it is a dream that dies hard.

Walter Clark's Frontier

Max Westbrook's little book *Walter van Tilburg Clark* (Twayne, 1969)—a book whose perceptions I often agree with, though its metaphysical terminology and its Zen-and-Jung dialectic leave me pretty confused—begins with an anecdote told by Walt Clark himself. He said he was once introduced to a lady in the East as the author of *The Ox-Bow Incident*. She was incredulous. "You wrote *that?* My God, I thought you'd been dead for fifty years. You know: Owen Wister and all those people."

It is an instructive story. For one thing, it demonstrates the swiftness with which *The Ox-Bow Incident* made its way onto the small shelf of Western classics. It further suggests that a book on that shelf is somehow embalmed. It has no contemporary reality to the ordinary reader; it acquires the remoteness and larger-than-life simplicities of myth and of certain kinds of folklore. And finally, as Westbrook points out, the lady made a common but serious error in relating *The Ox-Bow Incident* to *The Virginian*. It is like *The Virginian* in only superficial ways. Its purpose is not the celebration or even the definition of the cowboy hero whom Wister and Frederic Remington, between them, self-consciously created. To link it with Wister's belated chivalry is like comparing Conrad with Captain Marryat because both wrote about sailors. In actual fact, *The Ox-Bow Incident* is more in the vein of Henry James, that "historian of fine consciences," than of Wister.

I have just reread Walt Clark, all of him except the early poems and a few ephemeral essays. It was a too-brief pleasure, for he was a novelist for only a decade, from *The Ox-Bow Incident*, in 1940, to *The Track of the Cat*, in 1949, and from posterity's point of view he wrote only four books.

He and I were alike in our response to the country that bred us. We were Westerners in what desert, mountains, weather, and space meant to us. But I was much more limitedly a product of the young West than Walt Clark was. The civilized tradition of books, ideas, poetry, history, philosophy, all the instruments and residues of human self-examination, all the storage-and-retrieval possibilities of human experience, I knew only in school, and most imperfectly. I was a western boy who came hungrily toward civilization from the profound barbarism of the frontier, and was confronted with the fairly common task assigned American would-be writers: that of encompassing in one lifetime, from scratch, the total achievement of the race. Walt was luckier. He was a western boy who possessed civilization from childhood.

He grew up in a cultivated home, and his translation westward at the age of eight was not a move toward deprivation. His father was highly educated, the president of the University of Nevada; his mother was a gifted musician. Books, music, ideas that I discovered late and by accident, or never discovered at all, were Walt's from birth. He really possessed the two worlds of civilization and the West, where I had only the West, so that I became a kind of pretender, or at best a seeker, every morning when I left for school. He was light-years ahead of me in self-knowledge and awareness. When he sat down to write about the West he was not, like me, limited to writing about scrub oak or sagebrush and wishing they were the silver apples of the moon. He was self-consciously trying to graft the silver apples onto the sagebrush rootstock.

He consistently tried to make the past, including the spiritually healthy but largely unrecorded past of the displaced Indians, relate to the present. He repudiated the machismo that won and half ruined the West, but did not repudiate its energy. He wanted it reinformed with spirituality, art, respect for the earth, a knowledge of good and evil. He wanted the West to become a true civilization, not a ruthless occupation disguised as a romantic myth.

Civilization is Walter Clark's theme; the West is only his raw material. What else is the burden of *The Ox-Bow Incident?* That novel is a long way from being a simple reversal of the vigilante stereotype or an ironic questioning of vigilante justice. It is a probing of the whole blind ethics of an essentially false, imperfectly formed, excessively masculine society, and of the way in which individuals, out of personal inadequacy, out of mistaken loyalties and priorities, out of a fear of seeming to be womanish, or out of plain cowardice, let themselves be pushed into murder. We live mainly by forms and patterns, the novel says. If the forms are bad, we live badly. We have no problem telling where good and evil dwell when we are dealing with the Virginian and Trampas in Wister's book. But here you cannot tell them by the color of their hats. Neither the lynchers nor the lynched are all good guys or bad guys. Many of the lynchers would rather not be there and have not known how to say so. The hanged men are a greenhorn, a senile old man, and a Mexican no better than he should be. The terrified greenhorn, once he has accepted his situation, dies better than the Mexican, who was at first bold and unafraid. Davies, who opposed from the beginning the lynch mood of Tetley, failed to stop him because, quite simply, Tetley had more guts than he did. The preacher's morality is not binding, because it is imported, almost irrelevant. Evil has courage, good is sometimes cowardly, reality gets bent by appearances. And the book does not end with the discovery that the hanged men are innocent and that lynch law is a mistake. It goes on examining how *profound* a mistake. The moral ambiguities reverberate through the town. We begin to know the good guys from the bad guys by the way they deal with their own complicity in a tragic error. And the moral questioning, the first stage of conscience, goes on in the mind of that most Jamesian of cowboys, Art Croft, very much as it goes on in the consciousness of the nameless narrator of *The Nigger of the "Narcissus"* after the crew comes ashore.

I suspect that *The Ox-Bow Incident*'s unchallenged place on the shelf of Western classics is due not to its being fully appreciated and comprehended but to its persistently being misread as the kind of mythic Western Walt Clark was actually all but parodying. Look at the blurbs on the Signet paperback, and at the summary of the book on the first inside page. To Signet and Signet's readers, it is a novel of excitement and suspense and nervous trigger fingers. They do not read it as the report of a failure of individual and social conscience and nerve, an account of wrong sanctioned and forced by the false ethics of a barbarous folk culture. They do not read it as a lamentable episode of a civilization in the throes of being born.

Clark's adaptation of the Western makes use of its machinery but substitutes a complex and ambiguous moral problem for the blacks and whites of the genre. His version of the *Kunstroman* is equally desimplified. I call *The City of Trembling Leaves* (1945) a *Kunstroman* rather than a spiritual autobiography because, though there are unquestionably autobiographical elements in it, Clark has taken evasive action: has made Tim Hazard's family entirely unlike his own and has kept himself in the book, by name, as a commentator. These disguises do not keep me from believing that a good deal of Tim Hazard's pilgrimage was also Walt Clark's. There is much internal evidence, such as the preoccupation with the Tristan cycle, with tennis, with the purifications to be found in the mountains, with the presence of the watchful gods.

Never mind. Biography or autobiography, it belongs in the pigeonhole with *A Portrait of the Artist as a Young Man; Look Homeward, Angel; Wilhelm Meister; The Hill of Dreams*, and some more somber books such as *Jude the Obscure*, and especially some western American portraits of the artist such as *The Song of the Lark*. It chronicles the development of a sensitive adolescent into an artist. It is focused on the relation between art and life, that obsessive theme of Thomas Mann's, and it explores that relation not only through Tim's music and through the painting and sculpture of Lawrence Black but also through the several variations on artistic adjustment made by Tim's musician friends in Carmel. It reveals a skinless sensibility in its mystical feeling for Pyramid Lake, the Sierra, and the desert. It weds Tim Hazard to the physical universe by a rite of passage and a symbolic skinny-dip straight out of Frazer's *The Golden Bough*, or if you follow Max Westbrook's interpretation of Clark's writings, out of Jung. These are all fairly standard elements of a literary genre at least a hundred years old before Walter Clark took hold of it—a genre, one should note, often favored by self-obsessed romantics at war with their surroundings.

But if Tim Hazard is romantic, his book is not. It is steadily cauterized by irony. And the element of repudiation and compulsive self-exile, almost standard among spiritual autobiographies, is absolutely missing. Tim Hazard, this sensitive youth with musical aspirations and a high cultural potential, grows up in Reno, Nevada, and is never at war with it. It does not frustrate him. He hardly notices it, in fact, he is so absorbed in school, and girls, and running, and tennis, and playing in jazz bands. He accepts—and so did I—the standards of his time and place, and tries to star in what they value; and if he can't accept them he ignores them. His father and brother are not his kind, but he doesn't think of them as his enemies, or as threats to his spirit. Reno, in its double aspect of middle-class town and jackpot center, is not for him the threat that Dublin was to Joyce, or Asheville and his mother's boardinghouse were to Thomas Wolfe, or Wellington, New Zealand, was to Katherine Mansfield, or all of America was to Ezra Pound.

Most important, the end of his long struggle to be an artist is not exile or flight, as in so many lives and books, but reconciliation with his town and himself. Art ultimately leads him not away from his limited western American town, but deeper into it. He adds music to Reno without obliterating the traces of Reno that are left in himself. He is not led, as his friend

Lawrence Black is, to a self-destructive perfectionism, either. He does not consider himself contaminated by moving from dance bands to symphonies, from folk music to composition, and back again. Ultimately he simply incorporates the divergences of taste between himself and his town. Some things he outgrows, as he outgrows his adolescent adorations and excesses, but they have strengthened rather than harmed him. And that makes *The City of Trembling Leaves* unique in its genre. Clark has not justified himself at the expense of his surroundings, if we may take Tim to represent Clark. He has tried to use them to grow from, and in.

One must admit flaws in this novel. For me, at least, there is an excess of philosophical abstraction. And in trying to present Tim's adolescent adorations sympathetically but ironically, and at the same time not be ironic about the seriousness of Tim's efforts to make a unity of his divided heritage, Clark is sometimes overlong and unduly detailed, as if he feared the realistic boy might get lost under the symbolic artist.

It is an almost impossible task that he set himself, at this stage of the West's history, and it reminds me of another long, imperfect novel about an artist born in a little western town: Willa Cather's *The Song of the Lark*. But Willa Cather assumed that the American artist must escape the limitations of his birthplace, and be a stranger in the earth. When Clark lets Tim Hazard, after many failures, achieve his "Symphony of the Leaves" and settle down to live and work in Reno, he has dared to suggest that there is a possible reconciliation between serious art, the ordinariness of a little western city, and the primal gods of the earth. It is something I find hard to believe, but I would like to.

In *The Ox-Bow Incident*, Clark had suggested that the values of the frontier society were narrow, half formed, and in large measure false, and in the mind of the sensitive cowpuncher who was one of the lynchers, he had planted a civilizing seed of conscience and doubt and unrest, and hence growth. In *The City of Trembling Leaves* he proposed that a native western boy, given talent and motivation, might become an artist even in the unlikely arena of The Biggest Little City

on Earth, and might make commonplace origins serve art. In
The Track of the Cat, his third novel, he came in quite another way at the theme of civilization, the evil of the exploi-
tative and profane white culture, and the possibility of reconciliation between that culture's energies and the watchful gods
of the earth. Some reviewers were irresistibly reminded of Mel-
ville's white whale when they read about Clark's black mountain lion, and the book had a mixed reception. On rereading it,
I find myself willing to grant some of the objections but not to
grant that the flaws are fatal. In some ways, *The Track of the
Cat* may be Walter Clark's best book.

Objections on grounds of realism are valid enough. Mountain lions don't act the way Clark's cat acts, don't hunt men,
couldn't break the neck of a two-year-old steer, much less a
mature bull, much less two or three steers and a bull in one
flurry of killing. Only a lion given a heavy injection of literary
evil would act that way. Some readers would have liked it better if Clark had made his symbolic beast an old rogue grizzly,
the only animal possible to the Sierra Nevada that *could* break
the neck of a steer, and *might* stalk his hunter. Once more,
never mind. This is not a realistic story. And anyway, Keats
said Cortez, Shakespeare put a seacoast on Bohemia. This beast
is animate (and in good part imaginary) evil, and if the evil itself is made real to me, I am willing to suspend my disbelief in
its objective correlative.

George R. Stewart objected to precisely the sensitivity-
within-harshness, the literary transformation of surface realism,
that I have called a virtue in *The Ox-Bow Incident*. He insisted
that Arthur Bridges, the protagonist, son of a Nevada ranch
family, awakened by the bellowing of attacked steers, would
not have heard the sound "like muted horns a little out of
tune." That, Stewart said, came out of Walter Clark's sensibility, not out of the perceptions of Arthur Bridges.

Yes. Of course. I, too, would question that technical impropriety, that intrusion of the authorial mind, if I ran across it in
a student story. But Walter Clark was no student, and what his
authorial voice had to say was important. His Arthur is endowed with some of the prophetic mysticism and second sight

of Joe Sam, the family's Paiute hired man. Moreover, it is only
by peering over the shoulders of his characters and nudging us
occasionally with his own voice that Clark is able to steer us
among the tensions of his story and suggest the conflicts among
his generally inarticulate characters—between Curt and Joe
Sam, Curt and his brother Arthur, Gwen and the mother, all
the rest of the family and the drunken father. Love and hate,
good and evil, are as thick as the air in that ranch house. And I
keep remembering that one of Walt Clark's abiding intentions
was to naturalize sensitivity, subtlety, spirituality, modulated
and ambiguous ideas, in his realistic western settings. He chose
not to be limited by the verbal and spiritual vocabulary of
probability. So far as I am concerned, it is bad if he does it
badly, legitimate if he gets away with it. He gets away with it.

Especially in its early sections, *The Track of the Cat* is a
slow, tense drama, melodramatically lighted. For years, as a
teacher, I used it as a magnificent illustration of how to achieve
suspense by mere eyestrain. The characters are never overex-
plained; they reveal themselves in speech and act, and if their
creator's need to make them cast a long shadow sometimes
strains them toward some monomaniac excess, they are actually less strained in that way than some of the characters (the
preacher, say, or Tetley) in *The Ox-Bow Incident*, or the won-
derful, manic musician Knute Fenderson in *The City of Trembling Leaves*. Having granted the black panther a little legitimate heightening, we should not deny the same indulgence to
the human characters.

Symbolic, all of them, but for the most part persuasively real,
too. There is a real lion loose in the mountains, but the black
painter of evil lives in the ranch house. He lives in Curt, as
dominating and arrogant as the worst of the Ox-Bow lynchers;
and in Curt's mother, harshly pious, capable of suffering but in-
vulnerable to understanding; and to a lesser extent in Curt's
weak and evasive father. Their evil has already defeated the
gentle brother, Arthur, long before Curt finds Arthur's broken-
necked body in the snow. The same family evil—an evil that
we soon recognize as a regional evil, a social evil, an evil of attitude and spirit like the cowardice and mob impulse in *The*

Ox-Bow Incident—has completely destroyed the sister, Grace. The only one capable of resisting it, the only one of them, besides the defeated Arthur, who can make contact with the primitive survivor Joe Sam, is Hal, the youngest son. Most readers will identify themselves with Hal and feel his role as their own. It is hard to resist the temptation to be a culture hero. It is important to notice that Hal's position, his hopeful stance as combiner and reconciler, is the essential stance of Art Croft, too, and of Tim Hazard, and of Walter Clark.

I am perhaps eccentric in responding less to Curt's disintegration—evil destroying itself—than to the slow, tense drama of the ranch house. I feel Curt's disaster as a necessity of the plot rather than as a realistic probability. My experience with the Curts of the world does not lead me to think that either as persons or as symbols they are ever touched by the primal gods, that they ever comprehend good and evil, that they are very often visited by poetic justice. Curt at the end of this novel is something out of Eugene O'Neill, an Emperor Jones in chaps, where the others, heightened or not, are authentic. But I will put up with both him and the black panther—excesses of the literary and symbolizing imagination—in order to experience the believable, complex, human torments of that ranch family in a crisis.

All of Walter Clark's novels were written from ideas, I believe, especially from a preoccupation with problems of good and evil within the context of the real West. He was a little like Hawthorne in knowing all the time what he wanted to say. The characters he created to say it through, whether historical or contemporary, have most of the time a solidity and realism that are altogether admirable. If he had a weakness, it was that sometimes his ideas outran their realistic base, and he steered his people, or talked about them, instead of letting them act. Not often. And when the symbolic larger meanings emerge, as they do so often, from realities as solid as logs, when we meet and recognize the substance before we are asked to contemplate the shadow, then I follow him with my hat in my hand. He wasn't quite, like Hawthorne, trying to develop a usable past, or not that alone. He was trying, rather, to marry sensitivity and ideas to the half-primitive western life he knew. He kept trying to do the impossible, and he never missed it far. From 1949 on, many of us were waiting for the book that would outdo the three fine earlier books and cap the career. It never came. Why?

Some have guessed that teaching distracted him, and certainly he was a teacher incredibly generous with his time. But he was always a teacher, even while writing the earlier books. He taught in Vermont, in the Cazenovia (New York) High School, at the University of Montana, at San Francisco State, at Nevada, with shorter stints at Stanford, (Connecticut) Wesleyan, and perhaps other places. He wrote his three novels and his volume of short stories between the demands of teaching, and I can't believe that it was teaching that stopped him. Moreover, he told me in the early 1960s that he wrote all the time, and kept throwing away what he wrote. That was long after *The Track of the Cat.*

So did he, after all, fall victim to the perfectionism that he specifically repudiated in his character Lawrence Black? Possibly. What he had written had been widely misunderstood. His clash of belief and attitude with Leslie Fiedler at the University of Montana might have made him determined to say it in some way that even Fiedler could understand, and he might have become discouraged with the difficulty. It is likely that the dramatization of his difficulty, through the Fiedler episode and the challenge that Fiedler issued in such essays as "The Montana Face" would have made him more self-critical. And yet he was always self-critical. I cannot conceive that mere difficulty or misunderstanding would have silenced him or made him destroy his work.

What, then? I wish I knew. There is perhaps part of an answer suggested by the fact that from 1962 onward he devoted much of his creative time to editing the diaries of an obscure pioneer named Alfred Doten. To turn from fiction to history has been the tendency of scores of American writers who were reared on the thinly civilized frontiers. We have all done it, ever since Edward Eggleston started it in Indiana more than a hundred years ago. Once we have written the books that deal

with the early years of our region, or with our own growing up
to identity and awareness, we are likely to find neither the present nor the past rich enough to nourish the imagination. For
one thing, the western past has been sanitized by myth, and cut
off from the real past and real present. For another, both present and past are too new. The apparent maturity that comes
with the creation of valid literature about a new region is apparent only. Culturally, the first literature, even when it is fine,
may be premature, the product of importing a seasoned and organic tradition into an unseasoned place and society. And the
growing of a native tradition takes generations.

This is speculation only. I was speculating in those terms
years ago, and about others than Walter Clark. I had myself in
mind too. I looked at Bernard DeVoto, and Paul Horgan, and
A. B. Guthrie, and H. L. Davis, and other good western writers,
and I found them often slipping away from fiction and into
history, as if at a certain point in their careers they found that
they had done what their circumstances permitted, and had
now to start digging the foundations for the real cultural house
that would come only with time. In a sense, that is the history
of American literature, not merely of western literature. The
kind of cultural deprivation that Hawthorne and Henry James
lamented is not fatal, as witness their own careers. Neither is it
fatal in the West, in a newer time, as witness the strenuous
effort and real achievement of Walter Clark.

But without a more developed and cohesive society than the
West, in its short life and against all the handicaps of revolutionary change and dispersion, has been able to grow—and
without a native audience for its native arts—there may well
come a time in a writer's career when the clutch slips and the
gears will not take hold on the materials that are most one's
own.

If those things are true, or partly true, then it is under-
standable why Walter van Tilburg Clark's years as a novelist
should have been short. The remarkable thing is that he ren-
dered his own divided inheritance with such subtlety and skill,
and never took refuge in exile. His books are on the permanent
shelf, and I don't mean the shelf of mythic, easy, deluding

Westerns. His theme was civilization, and he recorded, indelibly, its first steps in a new country. He naturalized the struggle between good and evil in Nevada as surely as Robinson Jeffers naturalized tragedy on the Big Sur coast.

A Desert Shelf

Contemplating the opening of a great new library such as that at the University of Arizona in Tucson, one can easily be tempted into reassuring clichés. These are the occasions on which we are more or less expected to say the expected: to congratulate one another on the value of shared and cherished learning; to assert the durability of the highest human traditions in the face of ignorance, barbarism, and obscurantism; to celebrate the triumph of light over darkness. We tend to ignore the fact that only a small percentage of Americans cares at all about libraries or what they provide, and the fact that civilization seems to disintegrate at least as fast as it moves forward, and the further fact that culturally it seems our fate as Americans to go around in borrowed clothes or hardly any—that we are all a little like the immigrant who bragged, "When I first came to this country I didn't have a rag to my back, and now, praise be to the Lord, I'm just covered with 'em."

There is no organized opposition to the construction of libraries, as there is to the building of shopping centers and reclamation dams. Nobody has enunciated a no-growth policy in this area. So far as I know, library builders don't have to file environmental impact statements. Nevertheless, as the reluctant and minimum support of many public library systems indicates, there are those to whom such a library as this is a matter of the utmost indifference, and some who find the very idea of libraries objectionable.

The indifferent can hardly be galvanized. They include perhaps 90 percent of the population, the people who prefer dune buggies, skin flicks, and other forms of topless entertainment to books. Those who have philosophical objections to libraries belong to the 10 percent who might be expected to be on God's side. They include the vitalists, literary or hedonistic or both, as well as a whole spectrum of the antihistorical people who celebrate the present over the past and think they can tell one from the other.

Vitalists conceive libraries to be full of dust and mold. They perceive a great gulf between books and life. "Books are good enough in their own way," says Robert Louis Stevenson with some condescension, "but they are a mighty bloodless substitute for life." Similarly, it is only after he has managed to be "done with indoor complaints, libraries, querulous criticisms," that Walt Whitman can take to the open road. He appears to agree with Mr. Dooley, in whose opinion "Libries niver encouraged lithrachoor anny more than tombstones encourage livin."

Fair enough. Now and then most of us share these sentiments. But the antipathy of the literary to books is unreal; it represents only our irritation at pedantry and book-full blockheads. As for the theory that books are a bloodless substitute for life, sometimes the substitute is better than the real thing. When *Hustler* fell afoul of the censors in Cincinnati, its defense was that its explicit pictorial sex served a profound human need and was indeed a bloodless substitute for rape and sodomy. Whether the University of Arizona Library will therefore feel it must subscribe to *Hustler* is a librarian's problem, not mine.

The idlers, loafers, and soul-inviters that Stevenson and Whitman had in mind, as well as their contemporary hippie counterparts, are of course not book haters at all. They only pretend to be; they find it hard to be in favor of the traditional, and they resent the fact that libraries are housed indoors. But any expositor of Zen and the art of motorcycle maintenance is likely to have a book or two in his saddlebags—as likely as not overdue at some library. Whatever they may say in the heat of argument, these people understand that there is no dichotomy between life and books. Life is *in* books; books are in life. Eric

Hoffer, the longshoreman philosopher, spent his youth afoot
and perhaps lighthearted on the open road, working in the
crops up and down the West Coast. But he worked with a
copy of Pascal's *Pensées* in his pocket, and when working time
was over and winter ended the wandering, he kept warm physically and intellectually in the reading rooms of public libraries.
Books and libraries have been at least as important in Eric
Hoffer's life as paydays.

On the other hand, the antihistorical prejudice that half-
consciously disparages libraries as boneyards of the past is deep-
seated and of long duration. We are probably, except in cen-
tennial years, as ahistorical a people as the world ever saw.
Both the conditions of a new continent and the reasons why
people came to it encouraged a disregard of the past, and an ex-
panding technology based on science reinforced that tendency.
We mistrust the traditional, retool frequently, go culturally
stripped down for greater mobility, and equate change with
progress and life, custom with stasis, effeteness, and death.

John Wesley Powell, the first explorer of the Grand Canyon,
founder of some of the most useful scientific bureaus of the
federal government, and prophetic student of the West, declared that most of the record of the past is argument in defense of error. He was a most American American, and in his
way he was right. Librarians trying to keep up with a rapidly
changing science such as biology know what he was talking
about, for half of what they collect as indispensable one year is
disproved or outgrown or supplanted the next.

And it is not only as repositories of dead or useless or simply
unwanted knowledge that libraries go counter to American
prejudices. Being warehouses of history, they also contain and
in some degree perpetuate past injustices. They preserve copies
of *Huckleberry Finn*, which uses the word "nigger"; and copies
of *Oliver Twist* and *The Merchant of Venice*, which contain
offensive portraits of Jews; and copies of *Clarissa Harlowe*,
which not only records but takes for granted the degrading dependence of women. I know black activists who at least until
Roots could hardly be brought to say a good word for history or

the shelves that contain it. History is an enemy. Liberation lies forward, not back.

Those activists do not differ in their fundamental attitudes from the pilgrims who left Europe to found the Massachusetts Bay Colony, or the Mormons who fled the Pukes and mobbers of Illinois to create their Zion in the valleys of the mountains. The most exhilarating aspect of America was its promise of escape from repression, from past mistakes and unexpiated crimes, from old debts, from inherited slaveries and inferiorities. New Jerusalem, Jubilee, the Big Rock Candy Mountain, New Harmony, Brook Farm, the barefoot communes where long-haired saints grow organic vegetables, are all variants of the same dream, dreamed first in older countries and redreamed on successive frontiers of this one where it seemed to have a chance of coming true.

The New World encouraged the unloading of Europe, the symbolic act that D. H. Lawrence described as the killing of the father. But, from the beginning, some have been unwilling to kill the father, and others have found that he will not die. Cultures live on, either as debased residues or as abject imitations; there is no way to be new that does not reuse most of the elements of the old. Hence the ambivalence that a thousand observers have remarked in American civilization: its brash assertiveness on the one hand, and on the other its shamefaced acknowledgment of European cultural superiority.

A good part of American intellectual history has involved the attempt to rationalize the fusion of cultivated and crude, to define the new. I have been asking myself "Who am I?" since I was in the first grade. At the age of five I was carried off to Saskatchewan with the rest of the family baggage, which was not extensive, and on the way I lost not only my teddy bear but my country and my identity. Canada in 1914 was involved in World War I, and Canadian kids kept demanding of little immigrants why the United States was too yellow to get in and help. Almost the only fistfights I ever had were in defense of my country—my *old* country, now bewilderingly lost. I didn't know whether I was American or Canadian, or what it meant to be either. For a while, because my mother was of Norwegian parentage, I tried to be a Norwegian, and signed my school-books and my personal copy of *Tarzan of the Apes* with the family's old-country name. And when at the age of eleven I was taken out of Canada and back to Montana, and Montana kids snickered at my turtlenecked sweaters and my shoepac mocca-sins, then I was sick for home and for my short-lived Canadian identity, and half resentful of the one I was expected to re-sume.

We know ourselves not as idiosyncratic individuals but by our cultural heritage and affiliations—we do not exist without the language, history, political institutions, laws, customs, games, foods, and arts that shaped our growing up—and my her-itage was broken and my affiliations uncertain. Things would have been even more confusing if I had had to adapt to an-other language, but still I was a sort of quintessential Ameri-can, almost as abstract as an equation, culturally stripped for life in a primitive country. I was a good shot by the time I was ten, and had had a long course in the casual killing of crea-tures, which is the saddest consequence of any frontier, but I had never been in—had never heard mention of—a museum or a library, never been to a play or an opera or a concert, knew no music more advanced than dirty folksongs and Sunday-school hymns. I had never seen a picture more sophisticated than those on calendars or on the tin shields with which we used to close up the stovepipe holes when we dismantled the stoves in spring. Those chromos were mainly concerned with frontier confrontations: men in canoes coming around bends upon upreared grizzly bears.

The town we lived in in winter was five years younger than I was. The prairie homestead where we spent our summers was a sea of grass utterly unmarked by the Blackfeet and Assiniboines who had hunted and fought across it. I grew up in a state of nature, without history and with no civilization except the rudi-mentary or residual folk culture of a belated frontier. My child-hood companions were as raw and perhaps as confused as I was: cockney English, Canadians from Ontario, Scandinavians, Dukhobors, French-Indian half-breeds. Though we shared a limited experience—and it was a strong bond, I feel it yet for anyone who grew up in short-grass country—we took the imprint of the new country each in his own way, because each of us brought a different mixture to our naturalization.

Once, I spoke about this to the Association of Greek Writers in Athens, trying to explain America, which they conceived as some sort of monolith, some single definable thing. It was clear why they did so. In the poems of George Seferis, who had just won the Nobel Prize, as well as in Katzantzakis and other Greek writers, there is a strong and universal consciousness of what it means to be Greek. History clangs like bronze in Seferis' poems; the felt knowledge of a continuous past and present informs every line. For twenty-six centuries backward, a Greek poet can hear a language that is recognizably his own all the way from Linear B. The monuments and ruins, the sculpture, the vases, the dramas and the philosophical explorations are all his, as are the wars and the defeats. And back of the high civilization of the Classic period is the cruder, mixed, warring chaos out of which it was made, the times during which men and gods came as Phrygians or Minoans or Egyptians or Dorians, and stayed to become Greeks.

Those Greek writers must have been a little astonished to hear a man who had grown up without history come carrying culture back to Athens. Some of them said frankly that they envied me, for a glorious past can be a burden to a writer living in a diminished present. But I envied them more than they envied me, for what they had was what I had spent my life hopelessly trying to acquire.

We have been a melting pot, but the country is too big and various, and the time has been too short, for us to become one nation or one people or one kind. We are much closer to what the Canadians say they want: a mosaic, an anthology. I am a very different animal from Ernest Gaines, a black man born in Cajun Louisiana, or Scott Momaday, a Kiowa Indian brought up in the Jemez Pueblo, in New Mexico, and an even more different animal from Alfred Kazin, a Jewish American born and reared in New York. You are not much reminded of Momaday's *The Way to Rainy Mountain* or Gaines's *Autobiography of Miss Jane Pittman* when you read Kazin's *A*

Walker in the City, and none of the three will remind you
much of Wallace Stegner's *Wolf Willow.* But any one of those
books is as American as any other; all are attempts by American writers to uncover and know their inheritance and their
identity.

Tocqueville and other early students of the American experiment feared the leveling effects of an egalitarian society. They
were afraid that distinction would not be encouraged and
difference not be permitted, that the tyranny of the majority
would bring us to mediocrity and sameness. It has turned out
otherwise, in spite of MacDonald's hamburgers and other leveling forces. Someone described us as variety within a consensus.
Individuality asserts itself, geographic and ethnic variations persist, the regions go on creating related but markedly different
civilizations. Though we may look much the same to outsiders,
we thrive on our differences, and when the wind is south-
westerly we can tell a hawk from a handsaw, a native Arizonan
from a New Yorker or Bostonian or Georgian, a black American from a white one and an Indian American from either. As
for distinction, it can hardly be said to be suppressed when in
1976 this single nation sweeps the Nobel Prizes against the rest
of the world.

We still may be not quite sure what an American is. We
may never know. We are bound to go on trying to find out,
and we make our discoveries within the narrower limitations of
regional or ethnic subcultures.

We share a cultural pilgrimage, but it is a different pilgrimage, and with different timing, for each region. It began for
New England when the pilgrims came ashore at Plymouth
Rock, and for Utah when Brigham Young's advance wagons
emerged from the mouth of Emigration Canyon into the valley
of Great Salt Lake, and for Arizona when Father Kino ven-
tured into the Santa Cruz Valley to establish missions among
the Pima and Sobaipuri Indians. For people of European or
Asian or African background it invariably means giving up
much of the old, discovering and adapting to the new, and
eventually, perhaps after centuries, amalgamating old and new
into something truly new and with the capacity for life and

growth in it. For native Americans it has meant being inundated and overwhelmed, nearly destroyed, by the high-energy civilization and the superior numbers of the invaders—and out of that overwhelming, like people digging out from a mud slide, a difficult reemergence and reestablishment on top of what has overwhelmed them. In either case, cross-fertilization. The meeting of two cultures is a challenge that, even when one seems totally defeated, begets a living response.

A library such as Arizona's new facility is the storehouse of that amalgamation and cross-fertilization and adaptation. It is both a monument and an instrument. It binds Arizona and the Southwest to world civilization, assures it a place in the history of mind, at the same time that it encourages the process of regional self-definition.

It is better, they say, to collect a library than to inherit one. In practice, those who love books cannot avoid doing both. This library looks both backward and forward, and in both directions all the lights are green.

Ansel Adams
and the
Search for Perfection

"A photograph is made, not taken," Ansel Adams says, speaking lightly, as is his habit, throwing off wisdom amid a cloud of jokes, puns, limericks, and laughter. He can be serious, and fundamentally is, but his nature is ebullient and pyrotechnic, and even when he is most serious he is infectious rather than solemn.

A photograph is made, not taken. In that single statement are subsumed his more than fifty years in pursuit of excellence in photography: his exploration of its expressive possibilities; his mastery of its techniques, processes, practical chemistry, and physics; his development of the "zone system," which has taught tens of thousands to see like a camera and to visualize the finished print before they ever set shutter and lens; and his consistent effort to deal with photography as a fine art.

"The simple statement of the lens" is what he says he is after. But he is the first to insist that the lens can do nothing its operator does not make it do. It is as sensitive as he is, no more. Photography is not button-pushing; the camera does not make its pictures automatically, the way a lighthouse blinks its light. In a gamesome mood Ansel will sometimes play lighthouse, rotating slowly on his axis, now and then emitting a low, intense, foghorn moan, and at every full rotation gleaming upon the company with teeth and eyeballs that seem to project through the beard a beam visible for miles. That is fun, and also art, for the playfulness of genius is still genius. But it does not convey the essential Adams message. A photograph is made, not taken. A photograph is not an automatic recording, neither is it an accident. It is a concept, a vision of the world translated into shades of gray and communicated "in terms of simple devotion to the medium—a statement of the utmost clarity and perfection possible."

Having gone that far toward solemnity, Ansel is likely to add, with one of those laughs that shake down everything in the room, "And there's nothing worse than a brilliant image of a fuzzy concept."

Adams was converted to the brilliant image in 1930, when, in Taos, he looked at some negatives of Paul Strand's and saw in them a luminousness and clarity he had not believed could be captured by a camera. For years he had been in training to be a concert pianist, and was already teaching and performing; but photography had been an increasingly urgent diversion, and his patron, Albert Bender, of San Francisco, had been suggesting it to him as an artistic career. At Bender's instigation he had produced his *Parmelian Prints of the High Sierras*, and in 1930 he was in Taos for the fourth or fifth time, still under Bender's aegis, completing a book of photographs of Taos Pueblo, with text by Mary Austin, which was subsequently published by the Grabhorn Press. Mrs. Austin evidently thought of the book as essentially hers, with illustrations by Adams. She would be astonished to know what it is valued for—and at—now. Even in his formative years, Adams had a way of making accompanying texts, whether they were by Mary Austin, John Muir, or anyone else, look like mere decoration.

His formative period ended in Taos, which as Nancy Newhall has pointed out was his Paris and his Rome. What

Strand showed him hit him like Saul's vision on the road to Damascus. Indecision about his career was ended. He put aside not only the concert career but the soft focus, the atmospheric effects, and the simulation of painting that had marked many of his earlier photographs, and dedicated himself to "straight" photography, the uncompromising statement of the lens.

By 1932 he had had his first one-man show, and with Edward Weston, Imogen Cunningham, and others had founded Group f/64, whose inaugural exhibit at the De Young Museum, in San Francisco, was a benchmark in the establishment of photography as a legitimate and distinct art in which the camera is not a substitute brush but a way of seeing. Though f/64 held together only about a year (Adams and Weston both encouraged its breakup because they feared the formation of a coterie), neither Adams nor Weston, nor indeed any of the group, ever abandoned the ideal of precision and sharp focus that had been their reason for coming together, and whose influence persists.

His old friend Francis Farquhar, who as editor of the Sierra Club *Bulletin* published many of Adams's early writings and photographs, has remarked on how swiftly, once he saw his way, Adams achieved a reputation as one of the great photographers of the world. But no one should forget how long the apprenticeship actually was. From the time when he made his first photographs with a box Brownie in Yosemite in the summer of 1916, when he was fourteen years old, he had been an enthusiastic, precocious, and energetic amateur. In successive years, mostly during the summers when he traded the piano for the mountains, he developed into an increasingly able professional. Nevertheless, he did not make a negative that completely pleased him until he caught Banner Peak and Thousand Island Lake in a clearing storm in 1923—and that was seven years after his beginnings as a photographer. It was three years more before he made another negative that splendid: *Monolith: the Face of Half Dome*, so massive, serene, and eternal that it might be the throne of God. Those two still rank among the magnificent statements of his lens, but they were isolated peaks in a range of high competence. After the Taos revelation of 1930 he dedicated himself to the kind of perfection they had half accidentally achieved.

His training in music guided and greatly subtilized his development as an artist with the camera. It taught him to think of the negative as a score, and the print as the performance, and he transferred from music to photography the effort to achieve the purest clarity of tone. It also taught him that technique is of the essence. If you want to be a pianist, you practice seven or eight hours a day, until your keyboard technique is capable of everything you might demand of it. If you want to be a photographer, you practice until the camera is an extension of eye and hand; you seek the technical means to handle every expressive need. Though in music you deal in sound, in musical tones, and in photography you deal in light, in tones of brightness, perfection is as difficult and as much to be desired in one medium as in the other.

Perfection, he decided, meant the achievement of the artist's vision, which was not a merely visual perception but a complex act of perception and transference, a conception of the finished print bounded by enclosing lines and translated into tones of brightness from almost pure white to almost pure black. In nature, Adams points out, there are colors, brilliant or subtle, that the photographer must see as equivalents on the brightness scale of grays; and in nature there are—properly speaking—no forms, only shapes. Imagination transmutes shapes into forms, and technique painstakingly realizes the forms in the symbolic system of photographic art, so that a sheet of paper printed in values of gray can actually strike the viewer with more force and suggestiveness than would the natural objects from which it was made. It is Adams's gift to be able to intensify the emotional effect of visual experience. More than one visitor to the western scenes which Adams has made his own by an act of artistic preemption has complained that nothing looks so magnificent as an Adams photograph of it.

Not many photographers had ever taken photography with such seriousness as young Adams, and few if any had ever possessed his double gift of artistic vision and proficiency with all kinds of apparatus and machinery. In only a few years, he was acknowledged to be one of the most gifted technicians in the entire history of photography, and he has maintained his proficiency, constantly testing the art's ultimate possibilities, constantly experimenting, constantly refreshing and enlarging his skill. Even now, at long past seventy, he experiments all the time, though he has long since determined the capacity and usefulness of every existing sort of lens, filter, light meter, film, exposure technique, paper, developer, and darkroom process. His zone system, of exposing according to the placement of subject luminances on the exposure scale of the negative, has made the principles of sensitometry available to every tyro, and gone a long way toward eliminating the guesswork and "averaging" from exposure. But it is not a rigid system. The vision must always dictate the technique. He denies profanely that he is a Zone Buddhist.

What he has learned he has made available. His five books which together are called *Basic Photo*, as well as his *Polaroid Land Photography Manual* and the series of workshops and seminars that he began for *U. S. Camera* in Yosemite in 1940, renewed at the Museum of Modern Art, in New York, in 1945, and has conducted annually in Yosemite since 1946—all those continue to give practical and theoretical instruction to amateurs and professionals alike. In recent years he has added a series of workshops at the University of California, Santa Cruz. He has been artist and technician, teacher and consultant, and always a complete professional.

Yet having become probably the most skilled practitioner of his complex art, he values skill only for what it lets him do. "The excellence of the mechanics is taken for granted," he said, in commenting on the great mountain photographs of Vittorio Sella. He is not the sort of purist who will never tamper even slightly with negative or print—as though the camera's wink were the blink of God. He does spot his negatives and prints. But he is no trickster or gadgeteer. Despite his interest in the expansion of photographic possibility, which includes long service as a consultant to the Polaroid Corporation, he dislikes gadgetry and the photographic magazines whose purpose seems to be to persuade people that they can buy their way to artistry by multiplying equipment. Anyone who studies the photographic data Adams provides with his prints and books will discover that he habitually uses only two or three cameras and a few basic lenses and filters, together with the developers and papers he has found best. Limitation, he is convinced, breeds expertise; sometimes he longs for the old wet-plate process that made photographers work harder for their results. "I like to believe that if I found myself restricted to a simple box camera I could create a legitimate and expressive technique around it," he says, for "what the photographer sees, and what he says about what he sees, have far greater importance than the possession of mere mechanical equipment."

The arts have a reassuring way of corroborating one another. Joseph Conrad once similarly disparaged the mere gift of words, remarking that possession of a firearm did not necessarily make a hunter or warrior. And when he came to define the intention of his writing, in the celebrated preface to *The Nigger of the "Narcissus,"* he might have been speaking of photography, and out of the mouth of Ansel Adams. "My task which I am trying to achieve is . . . before all, to make you *see*. That—and no more—and it is everything."

It is legitimate to ask either writer or photographer, "See what?" as well as "See how?" No more than Conrad would Adams interpret the word "see" literally, as referring only to the "recording" of "reality." When Adams asks us to see, he is asking us to see *into*. His mysteries, like his shadows, are never totally black; ghostly textures of meaning lurk in them. His middle tones are rich with detail. His clouds and snow are almost never bleached white, and his skies are rarely bland. Almost as much as Paul Strand, he hates photographing on a "bald-headed" day.

There is a sense, he says, in which any picture is only a collection of brightnesses. But his brightnesses, high or low in the scale, are complex—he dislikes the violence of harsh, unmodulated contrasts—and they are somehow more than simply the light values that make up rocks, trees, and falling water.

They communicate a reverence for the forms of the world. Without yielding a particle of their precision and clarity, they tend always to become hymns to the strength, delicacy, and beauty of the earth. By the time we have examined a characteristic Adams print long enough to say with certainty, "I see," we mean that we not only see, we understand and feel.

Far from using his camera simply to record the external world in the way that is suggested by the cant phrase "photographic realism," Adams believes that as photography "approaches the simulation of reality it withdraws from the aesthetic experience of reality." That is one reason he prefers black and white to color. In black and white there is a cooler distance between the world and its symbolic representation. Black and white demands the act of artistic transformation; it does not allow the easy and vulgar effects he suggests in his ironic motto for color photographers: "If you can't make it good, make it red."

He is Whitmanesque in his affection for "the simpler things of the world, humbly or mystically seen." What he focuses on his ground glass is not a reproduction but a vision, an experience, and therefore it is, like all true art that I know anything about, to some extent a self-portrait. "A great photograph is a full expression of what one feels about what is being photographed . . . and is, thereby, a true expression of what one feels about life in its entirety." At the same time, his kind of photography is an art of "found objects," not of organization and manipulation and self-conscious composition. Composition for Adams, as it was for Edward Weston, is simply the best way of seeing. He will not tinker with a subject beyond removing extraneous objects, he works by natural light, and he rejects the excessive "dodging" and darkroom tricks that attempt to make bad negatives into good ones. The extent of his manipulation is whatever the negative or print demands in order to become what he previsualized. A magician of the darkroom, he will not use his magic to cheat, and by the same token he is unwilling to be at the mercy of someone else's incompetence or dishonesty. By preference he sells his photographs as prints or portfolios. When they are reproduced by printing processes, he stands over the printer—and he long ago learned enough about the printer's trade to instruct most professionals.

Any discussion of Adams's view of art and life comes around eventually to Alfred Stieglitz, whom he first met in 1933 and who in 1936 gave him a one-man show at An American Place— the first one-man show he had given a photographer since he introduced Paul Strand in 1917. Admiration of the kind that Adams felt for Stieglitz is always to some degree recognition of qualities the admirer already possesses in himself. Stieglitz corroborated Adams's perception of photography as a fine art, and set him an example of the highest personal and artistic integrity. No one, not even Strand, Georgia O'Keeffe, John Marin, and the people who had made Taos luminous for him at the end of the 1920s, had a stronger influence on him. When, in 1948, he published *Portfolio One*, he dedicated it to Stieglitz and took pains to speak of its twelve photographs in Stieglitz's own term, "equivalents." He wanted them understood as what both he and Stieglitz believed art should be, testimonials to "a spiritual identification with the world."

The belief is basic, and has not changed. There are no periods in Ansel Adams's work, though in recent years he has worked more with small cameras and with the Polaroid Land processes. As an artist, he found his way early, and has pursued the way he found. On his seventieth birthday, speaking at the Metropolitan Museum of Art, he reasserted the Stieglitz position as if forty years of artistic nihilism, experimentation, iconoclasm, cynicism, spiritual muckraking, and the arrogance of fashionable despairs had never intervened.

"I believe the artist can accomplish most on the agenda for survival by creating beauty, by setting examples of beauty in order, by emphasizing the concept of the essential dignity of the human mind and spirit. I believe, with Alfred Stieglitz, that art is the affirmation of life."

As a professional, Adams has photographed all sorts of things for no reason more artistic than that the interests of his clients demanded their reproduction. He does not apologize for that. When you hang out your shingle, you take what comes. More-

over, "the function of a photograph may be of the simplest
practical nature, or it may relate to a most personal and abstract emotion—the sincerity of intention and honesty of spirit
of the photographer can make any expression, no matter how
'practical,' valid and beautiful."

In fact, every now and then the chance that is an element in
all art, and especially in an art concerned with found objects,
can let a photographer transcend the practical limitations of a
job, and bring him face to face with something that he leaps to
interpret. Thus *Rails and Jet Trails* came out of an assignment
to record the history of northern California for the American
Trust Company, and *Mount Williamson* out of Adams's self-
imposed task of rendering justice to the Japanese-American in-
ternees at the Manzanar Relocation Camp. Accident favors the
prepared. When Hamlet said, "The readiness is all," he might
have been voicing a motto for photographers.

Nevertheless, though some of the great images were achieved
on journalistic jobs, it is not the professional Ansel Adams, who
can produce on order a superb book for American Trust or the
Bishop Bank of Hawaii or the University of California, who
justifies our profoundest attention. What concerns us is the artist who is unfailingly open to the experience of seeing, and seeing not only the shapes and brightnesses and beauties of the
world but "something intrinsic" below the surfaces. The artist
feels deeply about what he sees, he has a reverence for the earth
in all its variety, delicacy, and strength, but he is the absolute
reverse of effusive. He sees with such austerity, even severity,
that some have mistakenly called him cold. He has an incomparable technical expertness in communicating what he sees
and feels, and for half a century and more he has been making
photographs so plainly stamped with his personal artistry that
they hardly need his steeple-A signature on them. They have
taught thousands how to see; they have become household images; and when much art has been retreating into denial or crying out in pain and anger, they have steadily affirmed life.

That a great Adams photograph literally signs itself is due
partly to his qualities as seer and interpreter, but it would be

foolish to deny that his most characteristic subject matter has had a good deal to do with it too. He has photographed—greatly—in all sorts of places—Hawaii, New England, the Southwest, California, Alaska, the Canadian Rockies—and all sorts of subjects—faces, streets, houses, road signs, architectural details, industrial machinery, gravestones, the textures of weathered or charred wood, seascapes, landscapes, peeling bark and growing seaweed and hidden ferns and Gold Rush gingerbread —all sorts of shapes which the eye of the artist and the camera transmute into forms of beauty and meaning. Nevertheless, to many people he is the photographer par excellence of grand nature, especially but not exclusively mountains, and especially but not exclusively the Sierra Nevada, that "great Earth gesture" he has been interpreting since the age of fourteen.

The public that celebrates him only as a romantic nature photographer, a sort of photographic Bierstadt or Moran, does him a disservice. It ignores whole areas of his art, which is of extraordinary variety. (When the "Eloquent Light" exhibition was shown around the world in 1964, reviewers agreed that not a photographer in the world could have matched it either in sheer bulk or in the quality and variety of the images.) Admirers of nature photography, too, are not without a certain coterie impulse. They praise Adams for being a champion of conservation, which he is, and a celebrator of unspoiled wilderness, which he also is, but they do not always distinguish clearly between his qualities as environmentalist and his qualities as artist, or between his artistry and his subject matter. Conversely, the limited view of Adams as a nature photographer has led a few advocates of the faces-in-the-street and industrial-ugliness and human-predicament schools to disparage him as an old man of the mountains, a maker of glorified postcards, a western romantic who goes around reshooting scenes that W. H. Jackson and Timothy O'Sullivan did better a hundred years ago, and who is, if not indifferent to social injustice and human suffering, at least incapable of photographing humanity as passionately as he photographs cliffs and clouds and snow.

The "glorified postcard" charge needs no comment. Anyone

who can call an Ansel Adams photograph a postcard had better find a more plausible lifework than photographic criticism. Neither does the antihuman criticism carry any weight, not unless one wants to apply it also to Aeschylus and Bach. But there is a certain validity to the comments on the photographic portraits, or at least some of them.

Not even Adams's most fervent admirers have been able to make a persuasive case for one kind of portrait, the kind that Adams himself defends on grounds of artistic theory. One critic complains that he photographs rocks as if they were heads, and heads as if they were rocks, and allowing the need of criticism to turn a phrase, there is some truth in the remark. Adams does not believe that "expressiveness," as it is usually conceived, amounts to much. He is not a candid-camera man; he does not want to photograph grimaces, and his reasons are not unlike those that Lessing adduced for the blandness of the faces of the snake-strangled Laocoön and his sons. "I photograph heads as I would photograph sculpture," he has written. "The head or figure is clearly presented as an object. The edge, mass, texture of the skin and the general architecture of the face and form are revealed with great intensity. The expression—many possible expressions—are implied."

But either because viewers are obtuse or because the implied expressions do not come through, a few of the more formally posed portraits seem somewhat static and stony, rather like Roman herms, portraits of qualities rather than of people. Happily for such viewers as myself, many of the portraits are "expressive" in the best sense, and some of the more candid ones, such as that of Georgia O'Keeffe leering over her shoulder at a New Mexican guide, contradict the theory outright. It is simply too austere a theory for most of us; no purely photographic qualities of intensity, luminosity, purity of line, texture, or range of values are going to compensate for a face from which vivacity has been deliberately erased or muted.

Though some of the portraits do speak to us like church bells, they are a kind of photography that others have done just as well, and there is a degree of truth in the generalization that

Adams is less successful with people than with nature. With nature he is not only successful, he is in a class by himself. The observation from which both his few unfavorable critics and his most uncritical admirers take off is that he is, before all else, a poetic and mystical interpreter of nature, perhaps the greatest who ever cocked a camera. And many of his most impressive images do reflect nature in its grandest, most overwhelming, and most manless aspects.

Nature, one says, not scenery. Scenery for Adams is a dirty word, an invention of the tourist business, an oversized curio. Nature is something else. Scenery is for profit, nature is for reverence, and the fewer tracks of man there are in it, the better. "Man, in the contemplation of Nature, need not contemplate his external self," Adams says. With the single exception of *Skiing on Lembert Dome*, where the human figure (figures in some versions of the print) is there simply for the designs it makes, I cannot think of a single great Adams landscape in which a human figure appears, even for the usual purpose of scale. Scale, power, size, grandeur are achieved by other and more difficult means. It is as if man and his petty self-scrutiny had been shrunk back into the camera's eye; as if all subjective emotion were no more than a coating on the lens, a means of purer clarity of vision. Response is implied, like expression in the portraits; but what does not seem to me to work consistently in the formal portraits works powerfully in the landscapes.

Nature has been as strong an influence on Ansel Adams as it was on John Muir. He is a Westerner, an outdoorsman, a romantic, a mystic, and his art inevitably expresses him. Nature conditioned his boyhood, which he spent in a house overlooking the Golden Gate, exposed to sky and fog and Pacific storms and the dim shine of sea cliffs receding toward Point Reyes. Nature even shaped his face. When he was four, an aftershock of the 1906 San Francisco earthquake threw him down as he ran from the house into the garden, and his sharp, crooked, curious nose has tried to look over his left shoulder ever since.

Yosemite deepened what was already ingrained in him. He never recovered from the love affair that began in the summer of 1916. Four summers of his youth he spent caretaking the Sierra Club's Le Conte Memorial Lodge; several others saw him leading club mountaineering expeditions. In 1928 he literally married into Yosemite Valley when he married Virginia Best, daughter of Harry Best, a painter and concessioner of Best's Studio, in Yosemite National Park. In 1937 the Adamses moved to the Valley, and have maintained a home there and spent part of every year there for more than forty years. Even more than Muir, Adams has identified himself with Yosemite and the Sierra, and much of his most magnificent photography derives from there.

One has the impression that, though it was his experience in Santa Fe and Taos that taught him about self-conscious art, it was the Sierra Nevada that taught Adams to see, and conditioned what he would ever after see most vividly. Growing up in another part of the West, say Arizona or southern Utah, he would have had to come to terms with color, and like his friend Maynard Dixon might have been influenced by the radically different natural forms of the plateau country. But Yosemite, with its gray granite, cliff shadows, snow, clouds, dark coniferous forests, and light-stung rims, came first. It helped make him the black-and-white photographer he is. It taught him that even the deepest shadow has half-perceived forms, just as the purest snow or cloud will be pregnant with implicit shadows, and that all the world's wonder lies between nearly black and nearly white. Watching Yosemite Valley under sunlight, moonlight, skylight, starlight, stormlight, in greenery and in snow, changing with the passage of every cloud, he had to learn not only to see, but to find the photographic techniques that would capture such changefulness. There is no place in the world that could have shown him more eloquent contrasts: the poetry of ferns under a sheer half-mile cliff, the suddenness of dogwood bursting out from a dark wall of forest.

That was the beginning, and it remained the core, but Adams has added the whole West to it. He has been a migrant, taking off for the Canadian Rockies, Alaska, Hawaii, the Southwest, the desert, and coming in for periods of rest and consolidation to his bases in Yosemite, San Francisco, and in recent years Carmel. At seventy-odd he does not make many new negatives. His dehumidified storage vault in Carmel has files of hundreds that have never been printed, some of them perhaps as good as his best, and it will be the work of years to print and study them. But, for decades, there was hardly a mountain pass, a canyon, a desert sink or gulch or wash, that did not know his old Cadillac with the strong photographing platform on top and its insides full of white-painted equipment cases, tripods, sleeping bag, and camping gear. He still works hours that would destroy many men half his age. In the decades when he was stalking revelation through the stupendous empty places of the West, there were stretches when he hardly seemed to sleep, so open and eager was his eye to catch the miraculous moment or to visualize the combinations of form, scale, and texture that awaited only the transfiguring instant of light.

Photography is the art of miraculous instants—instants of expression, of composition, of gesture, or of light, depending on what kind of photography is going on. It is an art which often has to seize and fix what is already vanishing by the time it is perceived. Of all the varieties of photography, landscape, Adams believes, is the supreme test for the photographer. He has to *catch* the fortunate combination of earth, sky, and cloud —he can't compose or position them, nor does it help him much to move his own point of view. When dealing with near objects, he can achieve great changes by moving his camera a few inches; when photographing landscape he can often move it a hundred yards, or a half mile, and gain little. And there are problems of haze, low color saturation, scale. The camera must, in the small space of the print, convey the very presence of the scene. And finally there is the need to catch the moment when the light is, in Nancy Newhall's word, most "eloquent," and to expose before that moment is gone. To capture the moments when landscape is revealed under a light supernal in its vividness, the photographer must carry his trained sensibility around with him like a loaded and cocked gun. And also, like any hunter, he must sometimes have the patience to stalk.

Consider two of Adams's best-known images.

One he saw as he was driving back to Santa Fe at dusk and glanced over his shoulder at a village he was passing. The sun was down, but dull light still lay against the church and the adobe houses of the town, and on the faded white crosses of the graveyard. In the east, the full moon was well up above the snowy Sangre de Cristo range, and between mountains and moon a lens of stratus cloud floated high in the sunlight that had already left the earth. Sky, cloud, mountains, the long alluvial slope, the broken barranca, the town, the foreground of sagebrush flat, stretched in bands of bright and gray and dark from left to right. And almost dark, going as he looked.

He estimates that he had sixty seconds to stop, leap out, set up tripod and camera, guess the place on the brightness scale for which he wanted to expose (it was no guess, it was like knowing twelve times twelve), set shutter and lens, focus, and expose. Almost before he took the film from the camera, the light faded. But what he caught on that negative, called *Moonrise, Hernandez, New Mexico*, is not dark. It glows with a reserved, dusky clarity; it has the "illusion of light" that marks so many of Adams's great photographs. Only the most fantastic purist would complain that the cemetery crosses glow a more ghostly white, almost as if with a light of their own, than they could have had in the light he exposed by. The darkroom magician has interfered there. For this is not a reproduction of Hernandez, New Mexico, at dusky moonrise. It is a vision translated, a concept realized. And done in sixty seconds or less. "Sometimes," Adams says, "I think I do get to places just when God is ready to have somebody click the shutter."

Or take another, made in the same year, 1944. On the west side of the Owens Valley the land rolls once, a rock-and-sagebrush foothill, and then in one surge goes up ten thousand feet. Seen from the valley in winter, the escarpment is white with snow. The intermediate hill is dun or tan or mottled, depending on the light, and on its flank it wears a whitewashed brand, *LP*, to indicate that it belongs to Lone Pine High School. The Owens River flows along its foot through a belt of tall, leafless cottonwoods. In the foreground is a flat, yellow meadow, with horses grazing in it.

Made at any hour, in any light, it is a picture, a splendid snapshot, in spite of the documentary *LP*. Adams did not grab the image when he came upon it. He studied it, visualizing the finished print. He estimated it as it would appear in various directional lights. Then he went to dinner and to bed. In the chilly predawn blackness of the next morning, he came back. As he waited, clear gray sourceless light grew until it showed him the meadow with its shadowy horses, the mottled foothill, the impressive loom of the Sierra fault block. He set up the camera and went under the cloth; then he came out and waited. Eventually, the sun, breaking over the White Mountains to the eastward, lit and burned like a laser beam on the highest Sierra peak. He watched the pinkish light flood downward until nearly the whole face of the range was blazing with it. He went under the cloth and came out again, and waited.

Then another laser beam slipped past the eastern mountains and tangled itself in the tops of the cottonwoods in the left middle ground. The roll of foothills was still in shadow, the range coldly alight. Nearly at his own level the little smolder of sun grew in the cottonwood branches. He went under the cloth and watched awhile, and came out yet again. By then the light had burst past the leftward cottonwoods and was brightening other trees and a patch of meadow along the creek to the right. There was a horse grazing there. The light pooled behind the horse, turning it into a black cutout. Adams went under the cloth again, waited for the precise instant, and clicked the shutter.

The resulting image, called either *Winter Sunrise, Sierra Nevada,* or *Sierra Nevada from Lone Pine*, represents no seizing of the accidental moment. It was made by patient waiting for the instant that Adams knew must come. But just as surely as *Moonrise, Hernandez,* it is an authentic rendering of miracle. The sky beyond the range is slightly darkened to accentuate the drift of morning clouds. The white magnificence of the Sierra, shadowed with crags and gulches, ripples like a banner across the photograph. Below, as if propping it, the almost-black hill has just enough light on it to show the texture of sage and rock. And it wears no brand. The ugly man-track has been erased from the negative. Below the dark hill, as if we were watching it grow and brighten, the finger of dawn reaches into the meadow along the creekside. It comes like renewal, rebirth, reassurance. In a moment, as we watch, it will touch and warm the dark silhouette of the grazing horse, as any dawn might touch and warm any life.

I have that print on my wall in an enlargement of about two by three feet, a size that loses some of the brilliance of the image but better suggests the grand scale. I have looked at it, studied it, innumerable times, and every time I do so it lifts me. It is like hearing the choral movement of Beethoven's Ninth. Once again, darkness has been overtaken by light, as if an earth promise were being kept.

One returns to Conrad and his definition of the artist's aim:

> To arrest, for the space of a breath, the hands busy about the work of the earth, and compel men entranced by the sight of distant goals to glance for a moment at the surrounding vision of form and color, of sunshine and shadows: to make them pause for a look, for a sigh, for a smile—such is the aim, difficult and evanescent, and reserved only for the very few to achieve.

Among the few, Ansel Adams.

The Gift
of Wilderness

1.

Once, the story goes, a squirrel could have traveled from the Green Mountains of Vermont to the swamps below Jacksonville, or from Chesapeake Bay to the Mississippi, without ever setting foot to ground. A flea on that squirrel, if he got the right transfer, could have gone on to the Staked Plains of Texas, the Uinta Basin in Utah, the upper Green River in Wyoming, or the Judith Basin in Montana, without eating anything but buffalo. If the continent's fish had decided to hold a meeting, delegates could have started from places as far apart as the West Virginia mountains and Glacier National Park, Yellowstone and the Ozarks, the Sangre de Cristos and the Minnesota height of land, and arrived unimpeded and full of health at the convention center in New Orleans.

Once, as George R. Stewart observed, "from eastern ocean to western ocean, the land stretched away without names." It is covered now with the names we have imposed on it, and the names contain our history as the seed contains the tree.

They are borrowed from the usage of a hundred Stone Age tribes, as in Passamaquoddy, Wichita, Walla Walla. They commemorate explorers and early settlers, as in Duluth, Cooperstown, Houston. They honor Old World origins and imperial claims—New England, Virginia, Louisiana. They mark physiographic features—Detroit, Sault Sainte Marie, Rapid City—or reflect the piety of their founders—Santa Fe, St. Augustine, San Francisco. They remind us of the aspirations toward the good life and the perfected society that their namers brought from Europe—Philadelphia, Cincinnati, Communia. Sometimes a homely implement or weapon—Stirrup-Iron—or a battle. or other incident—Wounded Knee, Quietus—has marked land and map forever, or so we say, with its human associations. Sometimes the name of a place, corrupted by oral transmission or misappropriated from an Indian tongue without being understood, teases us with possibilities. What shall we make of Ticklenaked Pond?

In the process of taming and naming the continent, we produced an economy that was the envy of the world and a political system that despite its clanking has been the model for individual freedom. As a civilization, we have not been so universally admired. But, good and bad, we have put ourselves on the map, and most of us have felt good about what we have done. It used to be the standard, unanimous American brag that "thriving" and "bustling" cities and "prosperous" farms now occupy what only a few years before was howling wilderness. We could cite turnpikes, canals, steamboats smoking up the Hudson and the Mississippi, immense rafts of logs coming downriver from the Wisconsin and Minnesota pineries, and could say in pride, "Look what we've done!"

Some of those cities were worth founding, and those farms feed half the world. We have made the country support, at a high level, 220 million people. But also, after nearly five hundred years of "breaking" the wilderness, we have to acknowledge cut-over forests, deteriorated grasslands, eroding watersheds, decaying cities, proliferating slurbs, lakes and streams where fish can't live, air that periodically strangles us and periodically lets down acid rain. Instead of the wealth of wild creatures that once let every American feel his place in the web of life, we have remnant populations in refuges or in zoos; and some species, such as the passenger pigeons that once overwhelmed our senses with their millions, we do not have at all. We must go to Africa or the Arctic for the kind of experience that was once ours outside every frontier door. We have been fruitful, and multiplied; we have spread like ringworm from sea to sea and from the forty-ninth parallel to the Rio Grande; but in doing so we have plundered our living space. If we have loved the land fate gave us—and most of us did—we went on destroying it even while we loved it, until now we can point to many places we once pointed to in pride, and say with an appalled sense of complicity and guilt, "Look what we've done!"

But even though our environmental conscience has been made uneasy by a growing chorus of protest and warning that goes back well over a century to Thoreau, George Perkins Marsh, Muir, and John Wesley Powell, we can still be astonished by how fast it has happened, and look around us like Plains Indians wondering where the buffalo have gone. There has been some magic; they have disappeared into the ground.

The aware feel dismay, the unaware have not yet felt it. The continent has been tamed, but the average American's mind has not. Even yet there is a delusive spaciousness in our image of the continent, especially its western half where the names on the map are sparse. Free land—arable and habitable land—was pretty well gone by 1890, but the free land of the mind, the notions and assumptions bred into us by centuries of spaciousness and waste, will last a long time, and will more often be papered over than corrected. As it becomes harder to look forward to infinite promise, we either project our expectations into the new frontier of space, artificial and sterile and nonrenewable and incomprehensively expensive, or we convert the gilded future into the gilded past, warp expansive expectations into nostalgia for a golden age, sentimentalize the frontier and the frontier virtues into the grotesqueries of a Great Western Savings ad, and perpetuate our delusions with our myths.

For complex reasons, the western half of the country inherits the memory and assumes the dream. It is younger and less altered; its vast open spaces create the illusion of a continuing opportunity that its prevailing aridity prohibits. Also, much of it is federally owned, and we have grown accustomed to using it almost as freely as Americans once used the ownerless continent. Even the most protected places, national parks and wilderness areas and wild rivers, are available for many kinds of recreational and research use; and in the BLM lands and the national forests we hunt, fish, camp, hike, climb, hang-glide, and run around in dune buggies and ORV's without much hindrance or control. I am glad we can do those things, or at least some of them; but the practice indicates and perpetuates a state of mind. By universal assumption, the public lands are for public *use*. By a not altogether logical extension, the resources of the public lands—timber, grass, water, minerals—are for exploitation at cut rates. The Sagebrush Rebel who exclaimed angrily, "They've locked up that land so you can't do anything but look at it!" was speaking inaccurately, but he expressed a common point of view.

From the time when kings with tenuous imperial claims began parceling out grants to court favorites or to colonizing companies, we have operated on the notion that America is a country to be given away, or sold for a song, or appropriated by the first comer under squatters' rights. Who, during the California and later gold rushes, inquired about his right to pan a stream or dig a gravel bar or stake a claim? The gold rush was universal mass trespass that shortly created laws to legitimize itself. The mining industry has not retreated an inch from that original assumption, and a good part of the lumber industry and an important part of the cattle and sheep industries have retreated only a reluctant step or two. Contemporary squatters in the Alaska back country operate under the same unwritten law, and will be legitimized by the same processes. As Walter Webb has pointed out, only in America has the word "claim" come to mean a parcel of land.

There is another reason why the West, including Alaska, perpetuates the American dream or illusion. Americans have a centuries-old habit of dreaming westward. "Eastward I go only by force; but westward I go free," Thoreau wrote in 1862. "The future lies that way to me, and the earth seems more unexhausted and richer on that side. . . . I must walk toward Oregon, and not toward Europe." Actually, hope and the future had lain to the west for Europe, too, well before Columbus. Hence the Hesperides, the Fortunate Isles. "Going West," that World War I euphemism for dying, could not possibly have become a catch phrase with the direction reversed. Neither Europeans nor Americans can die eastward—the unknown lies the other way. Nor can they live and hope eastward, either. The grim history of the Golden Gate Bridge suggests the strength of the impulse to head west when hope is pinched out in other directions, and at the end of hope, in the face of the continent's last sunsets, to jump.

In America, it used to be said, the heavens are higher and the stars brighter; and it was easy to believe, as Thoreau did, that someday American achievements in literature, the arts, and the life of the mind would also reach higher than they had in constricted Europe. That amounted to a belief in the perfectibility and ultimately the superiority of the American character. "Else to what end does the world go on, and why was America discovered?"

It would be interesting to discuss that question with Thoreau now. The arts, literature, and the life of the mind have indeed done some flourishing in America since 1862, but it would be hard to make a case for the improvement of the American character. The land of opportunity that emancipated Americans and taught them freedom has been an enlargement for some, a trough for many. It has bred up rather more hogs than Emersons and Lincolns and Mark Twains and Ansel Adamses. It has opened the road to privilege along with the road to opportunity, and for millions, as population and wastefulness gained on resources, it has been a failed promise.

One would like to hear Thoreau on the subject of how long optimism, liberty, equality, faith in progress and perfectibility, even the indulgence of private and corporate greed, can survive the resource base that generated them. How long *does* freedom outlast riches? How long does democracy survive the shrinking of opportunity and the widening of the gap between rich and poor? What happens to the independent farmer and mechanic of our Jeffersonian illusion when the country, having wasted its bounty, begins to lose faith in itself? "America was promises," says an Archibald MacLeish poem written during the Great Depression. Indeed it was. There were largeness and hope in American lives so long as open continent stretched out ahead. (One example: Theodore Roosevelt's father founded an organization that before it was through shipped a hundred thousand homeless street children out of New York to new starts in the Middle West and beyond. Where would we send them now?) By now, the American dream even for the comparatively lucky may have shrunk to Edwin Land's ironic suggestion: an eight-hour day with two martinis at its end.

It has happened too fast for our minds to adjust to it. Thoreau believed that the woods around the Great Lakes would remain wilderness for many generations. They were leveled within forty years. Except for remnants like that in the Menominee Reservation, in Wisconsin, there are none of the old magnificent forests left in the Middle West. Or in the East, where the broad arrow of the king's navy took the first and best of the white pine, and mills and blister rust took the rest; where the chestnut is wiped out, and the elms are gone from nearly every common in New England. And what would Thoreau, an expert on lakes, make of Lake Erie, which until a few years ago was too polluted to support life, and which is only being brought back to semihealth by a concentrated, expensive struggle by citizens' groups and public agencies against the unreconstructed exponents of the American Way, the same folks who brought us the Love Canal?

Progress and perfectibility were concepts that rested easy on the American mind in 1862. They could be taken for granted as long as, in Jefferson's words, we were poor in labor and rich in land. But by 1930 or so, according to Walter Webb, the population of the United States was denser, even figuring in the open spaces of the West, than the population of Europe had been in 1500, when Europe began flowing westward toward the wide-open opportunities of the New World.

And that brings us, by a long, lugubrious detour, to the opportunities that are left us, and the choices that face us, at the beginning of the 1980s and the beginning of an administration that seems bent upon undoing all the environmental legislation of the past seventy-five years and turning us back to the damn-the-consequences practices that have left us, in all the ways of true civilization, poorer than people so naturally blessed have any right to be.

2.

For generations the machine and the garden have proposed contradictory goods to Americans. As the garden is more and more invaded, dug up, paved over, and polluted, we may, being adaptable, develop plastic lungs and stainless-steel bowels and learn to exist in the environment we have created for ourselves, as Stephen Benét's urban termites learned to sustain themselves on crumbs of steel and concrete. But it may also be that we will lose—are already losing?—touch with our humanity as we lose touch with the natural earth.

Secretary of the Interior James Watt and other believers in the machine seem to conceive of America as a warehouse packed with resources, and themselves as Hanson Loaders and Dempster Dumpsters with the duty of emptying it. Philosophers of the garden conceive America to be an intricate, interdependent organism of which man is not an irresponsible beneficiary but a living part, a participant who suffers and perhaps perishes if he mishandles too roughly the land, water, and air by which he lives, and extirpates ruthlessly the other species, plant or animal, that he thinks useless or inimical to his own welfare. Marcus Aurelius warned us about that sort of arrogance two thousand years ago. "What is bad for the beehive cannot be good for the bee."

Obviously I am on the side of the garden. Just as obviously, I think the struggle between garden and machine will go on until the species develops either wings or horns. But I believe the dwellers in the garden will hold their own to the extent that they will save remnants of the natural world by which we can save something of ourselves. We already feel the consequences of the other course in reduced health, increasing uglification, and decreasing sanity and joy in living. We begin to feel shortages and perceive the wisdom of conserving and the madness of continued reckless raids on our earth.

Many Americans—a majority if we may believe the polls— have it in their *blood* to be members and advocates of untrammeled nature. They don't need consequences to teach them. For while we were working so ruthlessly on the wilderness, it was working on us. It altered our habits, our cuisine, our language, our expectations, our images, our heroes. It put a curve in our axe helves and a bend in our religion. It built something into our national memory; it made us a promise. Obviously that change did not happen directly to every American, and new Americans who arrived too late to be rebaptized in wildness and who know no America except the asphalt jungles may hardly have felt it at all. But it happened to enough, and enough generations, so that institutions, laws, faiths, relations with the universe were given a torque that later Americans benefited by and learned from, that laws tend to conform themselves to, that is part of a native American faith. Many people who never or rarely get to enjoy wild nature have a belief in its rightness. That is why the "mandate" upon which Mr. Watt seems to count is inevitably going to blow up in his face. For obvious reasons, the characteristic American relation with the earth persists most strongly in the West, but it has by no means vanished from New England, the South, or the Midwest; and if only as echoes of half-forgotten history, or phrases from revolutionary declarations only half understood, or in the figures of our popular heroes, most of whom were wild men—if only in these secondary and derivative ways, it is part of the American tradition to feel a bond with the wildness which Thoreau said was the salvation of the world.

The very first archetypal American in our literature was Natty Bumppo, Leatherstocking. Cooper modeled him on Daniel Boone, and he captured not only the American but the European imagination: something new under the sun, part white Indian, part noble savage, totally removed from Europe and Europe's influence, a natural philosopher who saw God in the forest and mountains and prairie; and at the same time a loner and a killer, a symbolic orphan without antecedents: that new man, the American. He was created out of loneliness and isolation and total freedom and self-reliance; he had tested himself against a thousand dangers and perfected himself in a thousand skills. He was as self-sufficient as an Indian in the woods, and more formidable. Properly speaking, he belonged to no human society, as both Indians and whites commonly did, but was the Adam of a new one. Before ever Emerson proclaimed that we had listened too long to the courtly voice of Europe, Leatherstocking had forgotten that voice—rather, he had never heard it.

At the end of *The Pioneers*, the first novel in which he appeared, in 1823, Leatherstocking is driven out of the upstate New York settlements by the increasing of people and the diminishing of game and the tightening of civilized laws, and he goes where? West, where in the last of the Leatherstocking Tales, *The Prairie*, Cooper let him die in the light of a last blazing sunset, answering the call of the remoter wilderness with a firm, confident "Here!" Cooper was an antidemocrat and a writer of flatulent prose, but until Mark Twain created Huckleberry Finn, no American writer made a more persuasive portrait of an American in all his newness. Leatherstocking was the heroic model for a whole series of mythic figures built from history: Crockett, Carson, Bridger. In spite of our contemporary black humor and our antiheroic literary theories, he influences us yet. He is there in Hemingway's code heroes; he invests such contemporary masterpieces as Faulkner's "The Bear." He gives us some vision of our possibilities as Americans; he teaches us how wildness may alter us without turning us into bloodthirsty savages. It is not civilization that clings to his buckskins, but an innate nobility and decency, and he mistrusts destructive progress as much as any Sierra Clubber.

What remains of Leatherstocking in us remains often in distorted forms. One thing that survives is an intractable independence, an impatience with law and restriction. Unfortunately, that single trait marks many kinds. Sagebrush Rebels, members of motorcycle rallies and snowmobile organizations, and juveniles who test themselves against the police express it as surely as does a climber who tests his nerve and skill against

Grand Teton or El Capitan. We are a lawless nation partly because we have been a very free nation, undisciplined in the British sense. One remembers Mrs. Trollope's fretful remark that liberty in America is enjoyed by the disorderly at the expense of the orderly. Some part of Crèvecoeur's equation is still to be factored in. We still have to civilize liberty and independence, without obliterating them.

Curiously, it may be the love of wilderness that finally teaches us civilized responsibility, for wilderness, once our parent and teacher, has become our dependent.

"We are a remnant people in a remnant country," Wendell Berry has written. "We have used up the possibilities inherent in the youth of our nation; the new start in a new place with new vision and new hope. . . . We have come, or are coming fast, to the end of what we were given."

That is not quite so pessimistic a statement as it sounds. Berry himself, a Kentucky farmer-poet who farms his land with horses and laboriously restores eroded hillsides, depleted fields, and cutover woods, represents one sort of refusal to go on with the unsettling of America that he has eloquently exposed. He has made the turn that the New England Transcendentalists made long before him; he has joined nature instead of setting himself against it. And he knows as well as they did that respect for nature is indivisible. An old lady talking to her houseplants, a weekend gardener planting marigolds among his carrots and spinach, and a backpacker exultantly surveying a wilderness to whose highest point he has just won, are all on the same wavelength. In all of them, the religion of nature and the science of ecology meet. Though they may be Christians, they have left behind the Judeo-Christian tradition which puts man at the center of the universe and gives him dominion over the beasts of the field and the fowls of the air. America has taught them something besides the economics of liquidation and raid. In the same way that Indian names remain on the land, some of the Indian's reverence for the earth has become a part of us— some of us. I don't think it is an exaggeration to say that our health and even our survival as a civilization depend ultimately on how many of us learn that lesson. That means keeping alive and healthy not only our air and water but some parts of the natural continent, as many and as large parts as possible, so that nature in its wild aspects will be available to those capable of learning from it.

Once, in Hyderabad, in India, I saw a highway sign that instead of advertising some sort of goods or service made a simple statement: "Who planteth a tree is a friend of God." I believed that sign more than I believe most of ours. But I would add to it. Who preserveth a park is a friend of God. Who setteth aside a wilderness is a friend of God. Who preventeth more than the minimum of earth-moving and timber-cutting and water- and air-poisoning is a friend of God. And of man. Unamerican as his motivations may seem to Joseph Coors or James Watt, he may be the best American. He may mark the beginning of the end of the long dark ages of the American success story.

3.

Preservation of wilderness came late into our priorities. As Roderick Nash showed in his fine book *Wilderness and the American Mind*, our first perceptions of the New World had as much of fear as of fascination in them. William Bradford's bleak image of the New England coast, in which, "somer being done, all things stand upon them with a wetherbeaten face; and the whole countrie, full of woods and thickets, represented a wild and savage hiew," was characteristic. The woods, like Dante's *selva oscura*, were full of terror; we should not forget that the words *wilderness* and *bewilder* are related. Shakespeare, setting his last play on a West Indian island, made its sole inhabitant a misshapen monster whose name is an anagram for cannibal. Prospero's wilderness island is made habitable only by Prospero's magic, the arts of civilization.

But as Americans familiarized themselves with the wild woods and wild beasts and wild men they had come to, what had been fearsome to all began to be home to some. William Byrd by 1729 was exulting in the freedom of the North Carolina backwoods. Crèvecoeur, by the time of the Revolution, had begun to think of the wilderness and its tribes as a sanctuary from the furies of civilized war. Cooper by 1823 was able to conceive Leatherstocking, a man compounded of natural goodness and necessary ferocity, one who could feel the woods as nature's temples almost while he lifted a scalp. Thoreau by mid-century or earlier had gone all the way to a view of wilderness as not merely fundamentally friendly but inspiring. By the mid 1860s George Perkins Marsh, in *Man and Nature,* had laid the essential foundations of the modern science of ecology, and John Muir had adopted wilderness with a passion that suggested he was substituting it for the crabbed Christianity of his father. In little more than another decade John Wesley Powell would state the principles under which the arid West should be settled. And in 1872 the nation had made its first step toward correction of a long series of wrongs against the natural continent, and set aside Yellowstone National Park.

That was the initial act of a long, developing penance that eventually saved parks, forests, and wildlife sanctuaries. But it was not until the 1930s, as a result of the vision of Aldo Leopold and Bob Marshall, that preservation of wilderness for its own sake, without reference to scenery or to recreation in the usual sense, brought the development of the public conscience to its purest, least economically motivated expression. The first wilderness areas, from the Gila onward, were preserved only by administrative action of the Forest Service, and were vulnerable to administrative reversals of policy. But in 1964, after years of effort, the Wilderness Act was finally passed, and we began the systematic program of inventorying and preserving wilderness under law.

All the way, wilderness advocates have had to battle not only robber barons and resource companies but federal bureaus as well, especially the Forest Service, dedicated to Gifford Pinchot's dubious policy of use, which in later practice has meant cheap board feet for the loggers. They have also had to resist segments of the public bent on unrestricted hunting and off-road-vehicle use in the wildest backlands. Nevertheless, the 1960s and 1970s were decades of great progress in salvage and preservation. The year 1980 saw the Alaska Lands Act, that added millions of acres to our wildlife and wilderness areas and essentially doubled our national park system. It would have been a better act, with better chances of permanence, if the Reagan victory had not made environmentalists settle for what they could get.

How much of that century and more of intelligent land-use law the Reagan administration will leave us is a question that sobers everyone with a spiritual stake in America. For the preservation of the remnants of natural America, like the conserving of natural resources instead of exploiting them at once, offers America a physically and spiritually better future than the immediate cashing of our assets would. Just as it does not seem intelligent to put the California coast at risk for a week's crude oil, so it does not seem intelligent to invade our last wilderness sanctuaries in search of a little oil, gold, molybdenum, or other minerals that we will certainly need more in the future than we need them now.

4.

Once, writing in the interests of wilderness to a government commission, I quoted a letter from Sherwood Anderson to Waldo Frank, written in the 1920s. I think it is worth quoting again. "Is it not likely," Anderson wrote, "that when the country was new and men were often alone in the fields and forest they got a sense of bigness outside themselves that has now in some way been lost . . . ? I am old enough to remember tales that strengthen my belief in a deep semircligious influence that was formerly at work among our people. . . . I can remember old fellows in my home town speaking feelingly of an evening spent on the big empty plains. It had taken the shrillness out of them. They had learned the trick of quiet."

I have a teenaged granddaughter who recently returned from a month's Outward Bound exposure to something like wilderness in Death Valley, including three days alone, with water but no food, up on a slope of the Panamints. It is a not-unheard-of kind of initiation—Christ underwent it; Indian youths on the verge of manhood traditionally went off alone to receive their visions and acquire their adult names. I don't know if my granddaughter had any visions or heard the owl cry her name. I do know *she* cried some; and I know also that before it was over it was the greatest experience of her young life. She may have greater ones later on, but she will never quite get over this one.

It will probably take more than one exposure to teach her the full trick of quiet, but she knows now where to go to learn it, and she knows the mood to go in. She has felt that bigness outside herself; she has experienced the birth of awe. And if millions of Americans have not been so lucky as she, why, all the more reason to save intact some of the places to which those who are moved to do so may go, and grow by it. It might not be a bad idea to require that wilderness initiation of all American youth, as a substitute for military service.

I, too, have been one of the lucky ones. I spent my childhood and youth in wild, unsupervised places, and was awed very early, and never recovered. I think it must have happened first when I was five years old, in 1914, the year my family moved to the remote valley of the Frenchman River, in Saskatchewan. The town was not yet born—we were among the first fifty or so people assembled to create it. Beaver and muskrat swam in the river, and ermine, mink, coyotes, lynx, bobcats, rabbits, and birds inhabited the willow breaks. During my half dozen years there, I shot the rabbits and trapped the furbearers, as other frontier boys have done, and I can remember buying Canadian Victory Bonds, World War I vintage, with the proceeds from my trapline. I packed a gun before I was nine years old. But it is not my predatory experiences that I cherish. I regret them. What I most remember is certain moments, revelations, epiphanies, in which the sensuous little savage that I then was came face to face with the universe. And blinked.

I remember a night when I was very new there, when some cowboys from the Z-X hitched a team to a bobsled and hauled a string of us on our coasting sleds out to the Swift Current hill. They built a fire on the river ice above the ford, and we dragged our sleds to the top of the hill and shot down, blind with speed and snow, and warmed ourselves a minute at the fire, and plowed up the hill for another run.

It was a night of still cold, zero or so, with a full moon—a night of pure magic. I remember finding myself alone at the top of the hill, looking down at the dark moving spots of coasters, and the red fire with black figures around it down at the bottom. It isn't a memory so much as a vision—I don't remember it, I *see* it. I see the valley, and the curving course of the river with its scratches of leafless willows and its smothered bars. I see the moon reflecting upward from a reach of wind-blown clear ice, and the white hump of the hills, and the sky like polished metal, and the moon; and behind or in front of or mixed with the moonlight, pulsing with a kind of life, the paled, washed-out green and red of the northern lights.

I stood there by myself, my hands numb, my face stiff with cold, my nose running, and I felt very small and insignificant and quelled, but at the same time exalted. Greenland's icy mountains, and myself at their center, one little spark of suffering warmth in the midst of all that inhuman clarity.

And I remember that evening spent on the big empty plains that Sherwood Anderson wrote about. In June of 1915 my father took my brother and me with him in the wagon across fifty miles of unpeopled prairie to build a house on our homestead. We were heavily loaded, the wagon was heavy and the team light, and our mare Daisy had a young foal that had a hard time keeping up. All day we plodded across nearly trackless buffalo grass in dust and heat, under seige from mosquitoes and horseflies. We lunched beside a slough where in the shallow water we ignorantly chased and captured a couple of baby mallards. Before I let mine go, I felt the thumping of that wild little heart in my hands, and that taught me something too. Night overtook us, and we camped on the trail. Five gaunt coyotes watched us eat supper, and later serenaded us. I went to sleep to their music.

Then in the night I awoke, not knowing where I was. Strangeness flowed around me; there was a current of cool air, a whispering, a loom of darkness overhead. In panic I reared up on my elbow and found that I was sleeping beside my brother under the wagon, and that a night wind was breathing across me through the spokes of the wheel. It came from unimaginably far places, across a vast emptiness, below millions of polished stars. And yet its touch was soft, intimate, and reassuring, and my panic went away at once. That wind knew me. I knew it. Every once in a while, sixty-six years after that baptism in space and night and silence, wind across grassland can smell like that to me, as secret, perfumed, and soft, and tell me who I am.

It is an opportunity I wish every American could have. Having been born lucky, I wish we could expand the opportunities I benefited from, instead of extinguishing them. I wish we could establish a maximum system of wilderness preserves and then, by a mixture of protection and education, let all Americans learn to know their incomparable heritage and their unique identity.

We are the most various people anywhere, and every segment of us has to learn all anew the lessons both of democracy and conservation. The Laotian and Vietnamese refugees who in August 1980 were discovered poaching squirrels and pigeons in San Francisco's Golden Gate Park were Americans still suffering from the shock and deprivation of a war-blasted homeland, Americans on the road of learning how to be lucky and to conserve their luck. All of us are somewhere on a long arc between ecological ignorance and environmental responsibility. What freedom means is freedom to choose. What civilization means is some sense of *how* to choose, and among what options. If we choose badly or selfishly, we have, not always intentionally, violated the contract. On the strength of the most radical political document in human history, democracy assumes that all men are created equal and that given freedom they can learn to be better masters for themselves than any king or despot could be. But until we arrive at a land ethic that unites science, religion, and human feeling, the needs of the present and the claims of the future, Americans are constantly in danger of being what Aldo Leopold in an irritable moment called them: people remodeling the Alhambra with a bulldozer, and proud of their yardage.

If we conceive development to mean something beyond earth-moving, extraction, and denudation, America is one of the world's most undeveloped nations. But by its very premises, learned in wilderness, its citizens are the only proper source of controls, and the battle between short-range and long-range goals will be fought in the minds of individual citizens. Though it is entirely proper to have government agencies—and they have to be federal—to manage the residual wild places that we set aside for recreational, scientific, and spiritual reasons, they themselves have to be under citizen surveillance, for government agencies have been known to endanger the very things they ought to protect. It was San Francisco, after all, that dammed Hetch Hetchy, it was the Forest Service that granted permits to Disney Enterprises for the resortification of Mineral King, it is Los Angeles that is bleeding the Owens Valley dry and destroying Mono Lake, it is the Air Force that wants to install the MX Missile tracks under the Utah-Nevada desert and in an ecosystem barely hospitable to man create an environment as artificial, sterile, and impermanent as a space shuttle.

We need to learn to listen to the land, hear what it says, understand what it can and can't do over the long haul; what, especially in the West, it should not be asked to do. To learn such things, we have to have access to natural wild land. As our bulldozers prepare for the sixth century of our remodeling of this Alhambra, we could look forward to a better and more rewarding national life if we learned to renounce short-term profit, and practice working for the renewable health of our earth. Instead of easing air-pollution controls in order to postpone the education of the automobile industry; instead of opening our forests to greatly increased timber cutting; instead of running our national parks to please and profit the concessionaires; instead of violating our wilderness areas by allowing oil and mineral exploration with rigs and roads and seismic detonations, we might bear in mind what those precious places are: playgrounds, schoolrooms, laboratories, yes, but above all shrines, in which we can learn to know both the natural world and ourselves, and be at least half reconciled to what we see.